Praise

'In this book André Radmall offers the complete structure to help us delve into our life-story, it's influencing events and the emerging narrative that forms the person we tell ourselves we are. His decades of experience and insights are right here on the page, challenging us to transform our inner script.

    – **Carrie Grant MBE**

'André is a people-genius. He asks brilliantly insightful questions that lead to lightbulb moments. He has given me a greater understanding of myself, my assumptions and my reactions, which has ultimately led me to a greater freedom. May Andre's wisdom leap from the pages of this book and provide the same revelations and results for you.'

    – **Ali Martin**, Assistant Pastor, Soul Survivor Watford

'I'm continually astounded by the level of knowledge and spacious perspective that André has and am thrilled that he has collated and put together a summary of his thoughts in this book.'

    – **David Gyasi**, Actor/Producer

GET UNSTUCK

Change the Script, Change your Life

André Radmall

R^ethink

First published in Great Britain in 2021 by Rethink Press (www.rethinkpress.com)

Cover image © Bigstock | georgeeb22

Cover design created by Elysia Willis

Contents

Introduction

Do you need this book?

This bit could save you money and time. If the following criteria don't apply to you, feel free to pass on this book. But if you answer yes to two or more of these questions, you probably need this book.

Are you someone who:

- Feels stuck in one area (or more) of your life?

- Is at a turning point but doesn't know how to take the next step?

- Is in a situation where the old stories that once made sense of life have fallen apart?

- Can't stop repeating the same mistakes no matter how many times you resolve to never do *that* again?

- Wants to change but doesn't know how?

- Sometimes feels like a failure?

There's one consistent reason people reach out for coaching, counselling, a book or a class. It's a sense that there's something more – something beyond our familiar way of life – and they need a key to unlock that door. This book is exactly that kind of key.

People often seek help because of some form of disruption or increased dissatisfaction with the way life has always been. Our old narratives can be blown up by crises such as illness, a pandemic, loss or big change. They can also just wear out and become redundant as we go through life. When our old stories, the maps with which we navigate life, get disrupted or fall apart, we can feel lost, confused, purposeless and anxious. These are warning signs that the old roles and stories are failing and that it's time to create some new ones. At this point, you may for the first time start to question basic assumptions about life. At this point, a book like this may help.

I remember a client. Let's call her Sammy. When Sammy was growing up, her family would constantly tell her how clever and smart and pretty she was. She was told she could do anything she wanted with her life. Sammy went to law school and rapidly became one of the top corporate lawyers in London. She lived in leafy Hampstead, just by the park, with her husband, who was also a lawyer. They had two children and were happy. Sammy returned to work soon after each child was born but found she no longer garnered the same respect as previously. It started to feel as if she were standing still while others ran past her. Then one night, she returned home from work early to find her husband in bed with their childminder. One of the first things Sammy said to me in therapy was, 'How did I get so stuck?'

Sometimes, and I see this a lot in my therapy work, people realise their life has got stuck only when something goes wrong. Maybe someone dies, has sex outside a relationship or loses a job. Maybe the wheels fall off financially. Maybe someone gets sick. Any number of wake-up calls can alert us to the simple fact that whatever story we have about life no longer works. The old habits and ways of doing things that might have brought us success in the past are now failing, and however much we try to ignore this or make it right, we seem powerless over our own lives.

Many people might not even be in a crisis. They might have just got used to the status quo as they reconcile themselves to a life that might not be exciting but is at least predictable. They continue like this for years, maybe for most of their life. Then something happens that makes them sit up, look around and say to themselves, 'There has to be another way to live.' If you're at that point, this book is for you.

Have you got stuck in a predictable and boring life and occasionally think there must be more than this?

Or are you experiencing the chaos of disruption in which something has tipped your world over and you don't know how to pick up the pieces and make a new story to live by?

This book is for you.

How this book could change your life

This book will give you some tools, hacks and actions that can unlock your life. You'll find a unique blend of different approaches, including psychotherapy, drama-therapy, storytelling and acting theory. This powerful combination will help you understand the story you're unconsciously living out. It will also help you recreate your life story so that while it might still be rooted in your history, you'll no longer be defined by it. You're always free to step back into your own authenticity and choose the stories you want to tell with your life. Many people and businesses are living out the stories given to them by others as a result of circumstance or culture.

In this book, I'll show you how we can utilise the disruptions that inevitably put our view of life under pressure. Some call these disruptions the 'dark night of the soul' or the 'all is lost moment'. We can fear these crises and try to avoid them at all costs. But they can provide an opportunity to pivot into a new story – one that's often exactly the opposite to the one we've been telling ourselves, maybe all our lives. Let's look at an example from my own story where disruption led to change.

A few years ago, I was working as a self-employed psychotherapist. I had a good reputation. I derived satisfaction from my work and from seeing people recover from their toxic stories. But I had a feeling that something was missing. I was a middle-aged man whose children were leaving home for university, and my world was contracting into a predictable groove. In fact, my life was going round in circles. One day I was talking to a friend, a singer, and she asked me some questions about what I used to do. I told her that I'd been an actor, that I'd gone to drama school and worked in the theatre. As I spoke, I had the feeling that I was talking about someone else's life. Talking about my past brought up a dull, sad ache, like the memory of a lost love. I was surprised that even talking about this other life story was so overwhelming. I told my friend that I'd once considered writing a film or a play but that this was just a passing thought. I'd had to give up acting because I wasn't making enough money to support a young family. My relationship with my wife nearly broke under the pressure of my devotion to the work.

My friend kept probing. She wanted to know what had happened to that person who wanted nothing more than to perform. By this point, I was getting uncomfortable. A deep sense of loss and grief was starting to bubble up in me. I realised that my story about acting being toxic sounded thin and unconvincing. I'd been telling myself for years that the life and career I now had was the only sensible option. For financial, spiritual and relational reasons, it made sense to earn a living using my skills as a psychotherapist. After all, I'd invested many years and much money in training. I found the work satisfying and was good at it. My friend didn't let up. She asked what had happened to my creativity and passion for acting and drama. I ran out of answers. I saw that in giving up on my dream, I'd lost a part of myself. Worse, I'd mislabelled it as toxic.

A few weeks later I had another conversation with my friend. This time she asked me outright, 'Why don't you write a play? And why not star in it as well?' I had no defence. What I did have was a tsunami of feelings. It was like opening a cupboard and finding another me that had been in there for years, waiting in storage, and saying, 'Oh, there you are! What are you doing in there?' I was brought to tears by the prospect of returning to my field of dreams with this creative and inspired part of me. Of course, I was deploying creativity and energy as a therapist and teacher, and that was a real expression of my identity, but what I'd forgotten was that we can enact more than one story. These conversations with my friend sparked an idea for a play.

Within a year I'd written, produced and starred in my own show. The play got a four-star review in Time Out, which included the line 'If Radmall's future writing is as strong as this debut, he will be a talent to watch'.[1] This led to my making a series of short films, developing other projects for TV and theatre and starting a film production company. I've continued to work as a therapist and coach, and I've spoken around the world on the subject of transformation. But I've now reintegrated my creativity and passion for story. Before my friend spoke with me, I was sleepwalking through my life. I had a feeling that I was stuck but didn't know what I needed to do to change things. It took two conversations to wake me up to my own heart. These conversations were uncomfortable, emotional and a little disorientating. This is what happens when we shift from living our familiar story to reclaiming a deeper narrative that allows us to express our true heart.

There's one important and key difference between this book and all the other books out there on story. I have utilised skills I learned as an actor and dramatherapist to offer unique tools for putting new stories into action. It's never enough to change our thinking. That's step one. Step two is translating new thinking into new action. When a film director shoots a scene, he doesn't ask the actors to go into long discussions about their roles and the script. That's step one. When it comes to the film set or the stage, we have to move into the realm of people doing things, physically. Otherwise, all we have is a set

---

1   Time Out, *Dance Class* (Time Out Digital Limited, 2012),
      www.timeout.com/london/theatre/dance-class, accessed 3 May
      2021

of nice ideas but nothing to show for it. This book isn't just about creating new stories to live out. It's also about *how* to put the new stories into practice. If we don't do this, we'll constantly fall back into old patterns of relationship, work and life that just don't work any more.

This book is working from the assumption that we're all living out a story about who we are, what the world is like and how to relate to others. These stories are usually unconscious and unquestioned, but they're stories nonetheless and provide a version of reality. Over the years of working as a therapist and actor, I've realised that there's an infinite range of stories and roles that we can shift into. We don't need to learn how to do this – we do it all the time. We may behave one way with a parent, another way with our partner and another way with friends. We already have the ability to shift the roles we play and the stories we live.

I've developed a unique approach to consciously change the story using skills drawn from acting training, the principles of story and psychotherapy. A few years ago, I noticed that the skills I was learning as an actor and screenwriter addressed the same issues I was working on with clients as a therapist. After all, therapy is about understanding the story being lived and creating a better one. In other words, it's about not playing small. It's about becoming who we truly are.

The fastest way I know to get unstuck from the old story and jump into a new one is not via therapy or self-help. It's by taking on a new role and improvising a new life as that person. When I was at drama school, I'd see my fellow students make these imaginative and physical leaps several times a day. The beauty of this book, though, is that you don't need to go to drama classes or be 'creative' in this way to utilise the same principles and skills.

This book will teach you, in a practical way, how to change the roles, plots and stories that you're unconsciously living out. I'm not just talking big concepts here. I'm talking hands-on application. I've read tons of self-help books that are great at the conceptual level but whose ideas don't land in a way that you can put into action. However great the concepts, real and sustainable change only happens when these ideas are put into action. Acting training provides just this kind of bridge between concept and action, between story and role. This book offers practical tools for translating new thinking into new actions.

David was a man in his mid-sixties who came to England from Jamaica in the late 1950s. Although he was an infant when he arrived, he imbibed the hope and excitement of a family seeking a new life in the 'mother country'. David was reluctant about therapy, but his family had persuaded him to see me. He was a dapper, well-dressed man who epitomised the word *gentleman*. He was also lost and depressed. A social worker in an inner-city borough in London, he'd spent his career helping others and sacrificed his own needs to serve his community. Now he was retiring, and without his job, he'd lost his role. He'd lost his story. We discovered in the course of therapy that David had a deep story that he'd picked up from his parents: that he should be grateful to be a citizen of a country where he experienced casual racism and rejection. He'd made himself the servant of others in order to be acceptable. We explored how he could be valued in new ways. It turned out that David was a good drummer and had a secret desire to play in a band. This was an exciting idea, but David still had to take action. So he brought a drum kit and started playing with some friends at a local social club. It wasn't until his first gig that the story really changed. I still remember his huge smile in our first session after his first concert.

I'm not just going to teach you how to swap one story for another. I'm going to show you how shifting out of the old stories and into new identities frees you to be yourself, to widen and deepen the range of what it means to be you. As we let go of trying to control life with old stories, we can begin to live from the heart. From that place, we can create and live new stories rooted in love, joy and peace. I'm not saying that a human is a shapeless mirage wearing different masks and personas. I'm saying we can drop into our hearts and bodies and find a freedom to express what we find there.

This book isn't simply about helping you tell different stories and play different roles. It's about helping you break through some of your worst moments to gain access to a power and freedom that has always lain dormant within you. This book could change your life, and not just by broadening your range of self-expression and creativity. That alone is a game changer, certainly. But the ideas in this book could also enable you to bring all parts of yourself online in a way that is deep, powerful and authentic. As your life changes, you'll also become a catalyst for change in your family, your community, your business and the world. No one is an island – any change, anywhere, will trigger a domino effect that changes those around you. This kind of change makes the world a more loving, compassionate and caring place. So this book could change your life, but unless that change serves the wider world, it's still only partial.

My story

I've been through the despair of feeling unwanted, useless and invisible. I grew up in a family I never felt a part of and withdrew into my own bubble from an early age. I was adopted as a baby and any sense of alienation or isolation was perpetuated by a rather cold and repressed family. I was haunted by a feeling of loneliness and rejection. I tried to manage this terrible feeling of being alone by grabbing hold of TV, food, porn, alcohol, the approval of others and fantasy literature.

But

My darkness has guided me into light. My feelings of being an outsider enable me to see the world from a unique perspective. Disconnection has enabled me to learn the mechanics of building relationships from the ground up. Addictive habits have enabled me to surrender and accept that I'll never be able to fix myself without help from what I call a higher power. My feeling unwanted and invisible sparked the performing spirit within me and literally propelled me into the spotlight of the theatre.

My story is all about pivoting from dark to light, from a narrative of despair to a story of hope and joy.

Let me tell you my story in two ways.

Dark story

In the spring of 1961, my mother got pregnant. She lived in a small mining town in the North of England where everyone knew each other's business. Gossip and shame were the lingua franca. Having a child outside of wedlock was a sure-fire route to social rejection. My mother told her guilty secret to her mother and a best friend. Within weeks, she was in Jersey working as a maid. Like other women with her background at that time, she planned to give birth, have the baby adopted and return to home with no one any the wiser. But my mother deviated from the script and never, ever went home. She set up her own business running a guest house, got married to a local man, had another son and died of ovarian cancer at forty-two. As for me, I was left in the care of nurses in a cottage hospital for two weeks until my new parents came to take me home.

I grew up, not knowing I was adopted, in a middle-class home with elderly parents whom I never connected with. I lived in a bubble of isolation and fear, spending hours playing with toy soldiers, collecting stamps and listening to *The Archers*. My teenage years were coloured by bouts of debilitating asthma and dreams of being a rock star. When I was sixteen, my adoptive mother died of cancer. At the time, I felt a heavy cloud had been lifted. She'd been a dark and joyless presence at odds with my teenage preoccupations with sex, music and being intense.

When I was seventeen, my father sat me down in the beige lounge of our 1970s home and told me that I was adopted. Hearing this news wasn't shocking. It explained my feeling of disconnection from my family, so my overall reaction was one of relief. Something behind the scenes had always been fundamentally out of joint and now I knew why. I hoped that somewhere out there was another mother who would love me and lead me out of my grey suburban fog and into the sunny uplands of a cool, bohemian family. It took me nearly twenty years to find the courage to test that fantasy. When I did, I discovered that my mother had died long ago, about the same time as I was getting married. If I'd gone looking for her at seventeen, I might have found her.

This is my origin story. Like all origin stories, it's not only about historical events. It's about how I reacted to those events, the story I told about them and how I lived out that story. My reactions were spun around a constellation of rejection, fear of abandonment, hiding and the comforts of imagination. I obsessed over perceived threats of rejection and found love, intimacy and acceptance almost impossible to access. For many years I read the events of my life through the filter of these reactions.

Our life stories have the power of unquestioned truth because they're rooted in real events that make an impact on us. These events can even be traumatic. This has the effect of fixing the story in place, like nailing a painting on a wall. And from then on, all we see is that painting. This was my origin story. We could call this a non-fictional story, although it was certainly constructed and made up.

Light story

Inside every dark story are the seeds of a potential but as-yet-untold story. The light story.

The arid landscape of my childhood and the long periods I spent pinned to my bed by asthma provided a rich foundation for my imagination to flourish. My ability to be creative was never diminished by my external problems. Maybe it was even inspired by them. I drank deep from stories such as CS Lewis's *Chronicles of Narnia*. Sometimes the worlds I discovered in these pages carried far more meaning for me than my 'real' life. Like all the best stories, these fictional narratives weren't just escapism – they offered a rehearsal for living a different life. Stories showed me there was another way to live, out there, on Mars or in New York. I was so relieved to discover worlds beyond the outer limits of my neurotic and brittle family. Stories opened the window of my imagination to new possibilities far beyond the story I was living day-to-day. Books were my way out of a middle-class, middle-England bubble. I would gaze at the looping New York skyline in cartoons and ache to enter that exotic urban jungle of Manhattan. American comics had the sweet, musty scent of... America!

TV-show stories were also important to me. I'd lose my temper if we were out shopping and I couldn't get back home in time for my favourite TV show. I was a child with access to my imagination and the ability to try out different roles. I remember pretending to be characters from *Thunderbirds* in the playground of my infant school and how empowering that was.

Stories helped me find meaning and sense in a frightening and oppressive world. Stories held me together in ways family couldn't.

Stories helped me piece together a bigger, richer narrative. Stories held the broken pieces together. Stories showed me that good wins out over evil and that there's always hope. Stories gave me a lens through which to understand the world, and the creative juice to dream of changing it. This is why I wrote poems, songs and stories from a young age. Intuitively I knew that story could not only reshape my reality but also keep me in touch with my heart.

I always dreamed of being a performer, and eventually I found my way to drama school. There, I learned the craft of not only reading stories but also enacting and inhabiting them. I experienced the alchemic transformation of story into action for stage or film. I found it hugely liberating to be a Restoration fop, a Shakespearian prince or a Chekhovian schoolteacher. I'd watched these identity shifts for years in film, TV and books, but now I got to physically step onto the stage and inhabit these other worlds. I'll come back to this point frequently. Real and sustainable change happens when imagination and creativity are embodied in action and interaction.

As well as inspiring me to enter the world of acting, my 'dark story' also propelled me into a lifetime of curiosity about human beings and relationships. When I was nineteen, this enquiry took the form of my studying mental-health nursing and subsequently getting master's degrees in dramatherapy and psychotherapy. I've had a successful private practice for over thirty years. Throughout this time, I've worked in prestigious Harley Street, London, and managed an eating disorders unit at the Priory Hospital. I've appeared as a psychological expert on BBC Radio and on TV. I've contributed to articles on well-being and mental health that have appeared in publications such as the *Independent* and *Metro*. I've run workshops around the world on different aspects of mental health. And yet, my origin story of isolation and anxiety would seem the worst kind of preparation for the life I've led. I have also developed a spiritual life in the Christian tradition. Once again this has been an exploration into the deeper meaning of life. This aspect of my journey culminated in me being ordained as a priest a few years ago.

I believe that our dark stories can be changed into stories and lives of light. I've probably learned this the hard way. Over the years, I've tried many different ways to 'fix' myself and my broken story, but ultimately I had to pivot through my own darkness and into a narrative and persona that was always inside me. The creative approaches we'll discuss in this book don't take you 'out' of yourself. They tap into the vast potential within that has always been there, buried under layers of redundant stories.

I've been in several forms of therapy for years, gone to 'healing' church conferences and read many books on psychology and self-help. And I've experienced benefits from all these things. I certainly don't wish to discourage anyone from entering therapy, coaching or self-help programmes. But for me, the key changes have come through the approach outlined in this book. And this approach has proven helpful in different cultures and countries and with organisations as well as individuals.

A final note

In this book, I offer stories about clients. Anonymity is protected. This means that not only have the names of the clients been changed, but I've also amalgamated aspects of various clients into composite cases. I've also taken creative licence with many of the details. This does not, however, make these examples untrue.

ACT ONE
MAKING STORIES

ONE

Story Outline

*S*tory has become a buzzword in the fields of coaching and therapy. To get unstuck from our old life stories and build new ones, first we need to understand what the word *story* means.

Order, disorder, reorder

A caterpillar goes through a three-stage process to become a butterfly: order, disorder and reorder. In the disorder stage, the chrysalis stage, everything changes. All structure breaks down, and it's out of this messiness that the butterfly emerges. Similarly, a three-stage process can be found in many stories. As well as being a template for story, this process is evident during any deep and lasting transformation. It's the same for a client who's being coached as it is for an actor learning a new role. There's the order of the familiar (even if it's problematic), the disorder of change and the reorder of new life.

When I was working as an actor, I'd go into the rehearsal process as my normal self and come out of it transformed. I'd leave my habitual ways of doing things behind and enter the unfamiliar world of the story and character. It was, in itself, a journey. It meant trying out lots of different things to learn my role and place in the new story. The final shift came at the point of performance, where I'd enter a more ordered or reordered phase. My role would be different from my usual everyday persona, but it wouldn't embody the confusion, chaos and experimental elements of the disorder phase. This three-stage process tends to mirror the three-act structure of theatre and film. It's worth seeing it in these terms because in our culture, we often try to go directly from order to reorder and skip disorder. Advertisements and social media often promise a shortcut to reorder. But in many stories, all three stages are necessary.

A more developed version of this process is the hero's journey as described by the anthropologist Joseph Campbell[2] and since adapted by screenwriting gurus

---

2 J Campbell, *The Hero's Journey: Joseph Campbell on his life and work* (New World Library, 2014)

such as Chris Vogler.[3] In essence, a hero goes on a journey to achieve a goal or win a prize. This usually means going deep into themselves and far from their home territory. The second half of this kind of story is about the hero's struggle against the odds to return from the abyss and their 'all is lost' moment to take home their hard-won prize.

This is largely a male-orientated story and lends itself to many genres. In recent years, a more female perspective has been devised by writers such as Kim Hudson.[4] In this approach to story, the heroine moves in and out of her usual context and role – she moves in and out of disorder while trying to maintain the appearance of order for the sake of not destabilising others. She gradually realises that she's becoming more powerful and influential than she is in her normal context. Her dilemma is that she doesn't want to disrupt her normal and usually limited role and narrative. But over time, she cannot hide the person she has become, and her home context must accommodate and integrate her as the person she really is. This person evolves in the process of disorder that transgresses the usual way of being.

The heroine-type story is rooted in relationships and is really the story of relationship change. This not only

---

3   C Vogler, *The Writer's Journey: Mythic structure for writers* (Michael Wiese Publications, 2020)

4   K Hudson, *The Virgin's Promise: Writing stories of feminine creative, spiritual, and sexual awakening* (Michael Wiese Publications, 2009)

applies to the relationships of the person with others but also with themselves. In the hero story, the focus is more ego based, with the heroine seeking their own ends and doing it in a less collaborative way.

In both these approaches, the disorder phase leads to fundamental changes to the heroine's identity and her relationship with others and, most importantly, herself. No one goes through this three-stage process without their origin story being transformed and their potential self being revealed.

The potential self isn't the self we construct in response to life in order to cope, to get what we need or to just survive. The process of changing our story is one of surrendering the self-made self. Reordering takes us into a different state of being, where we're less defined by past stories and the ways of thinking that go with them. This is a bit like finding a clearing in a forest rather than being lost in the woods. It's from here that we can find freedom to participate in the creative and spiritual flow of the universe.

Three-act structure

Here's another take on the order-disorder-reorder process that I'm borrowing from the theatre.

In drama, stories move through a sequence. At its simplest, this could be described as the beginning, the middle and the end. When I'm writing screenplays, I'm thinking of this sequence in the language of Acts 1, 2 and 3.

Throughout I will be using the word 'hero' to apply to all genders.

Act 1

This is all about the normal life of our hero before the new story begins – basically the old story, which has been formed in reaction to the ups and downs of life. In Act 1, we learn where our hero works, who's in their family and just generally what normal life looks like for them. The hero may or may not be happy, but what we see at the story's beginning is normality. What's your normality?

The next step is what I call a trigger incident. This is the moment when something unusual or unexpected happens. The event could be small or big. It's some kind of disruption. For my clients, trigger incidents can be anything from starting a new relationship to changing schools to moving to a new city or job. What these trigger incidents have in common is a sense that normality is slipping away and something has to be done.

At first, our hero may try to ignore it, avoid it or make light of it, but the trigger incident has lit the blue touchpaper. This event causes our hero to want something and to start pursuing something. Inherent in this challenge is an objective to be achieved. All stories are trying to achieve something. This is the motivation that gets you up in the morning and moves you through your day. In a romcom, the trigger incident may be the arrival of a new person in the life of the hero. As he falls in love with them, he has a challenge. Maybe it's how to get with this person when they don't even see him. The objective is to start a relationship. Because he's fallen in love, he can't avoid the challenge.

In other forms of story, the personal-development narrative, for example, the aim might be to embrace a new life or identity. Paradoxically, this new life actually reveals something about the character that was there all along, waiting to be realised and expressed. The story of Cinderella is an example of this.

In this kind of story, the hero is increasingly changed by the objective they pursue. Superficially the change they want to achieve is a surface objective, such as 'getting the girl'. But in all good stories there's also an internal objective inside the hero. Often the internal objective is unconscious. So to get the girl, maybe the boy must come to terms with his own fear of rejection and avoidance of being hurt. The film *Good Will Hunting* is a good example of this. It's quite common in stories of transformation for the hero to face their own shadow, those feelings and parts of themselves that they usually suppress or avoid. It's in integrating these cut-off parts of oneself that the transformation happens. This is the energy that drives stories forward, and it's not just about transformation but also healing.

Almost all the people who come to see me for therapy or coaching are in Act 1. Something has disrupted their lives, and the old story they've been living isn't helping them to deal with it. All the usual tactics are failing, so they want to explore building a new story to help them move forward and resolve the disruption.

Have you experienced a disruptive, triggering incident?

Are you trying to do the things that usually work but finding that nothing is resolving the upheaval you feel?

If so, you're in a great place to move into Act 2 in the story. This will require you to step out of the familiar, if uncomfortable, territory of Act 1 and onto an unknown path.

Act 2

Act 2 takes up 70% of most stories. This is the journey the hero takes to achieve their goal. Usually they meet stronger and stronger resistance along the way, and it culminates in their coming to a point where they lose or risk losing everything, even their lives. In the middle of Act 2 there might be a transcendent revelation of the bigger picture. Part of this is an awakening to who they really are and their full potential. Suddenly the world looks different. There's been a perspective shift. The old life is far away now, and the hero has found the hidden treasure they seek. But remaining in this place of transformation means letting go of the old life. They've gone into the dark country of their own hearts and found unfamiliar landscapes. The old identity is shifting and changing.

With this new-found awareness, the hero steps forward to overcome the forces that stand in the way of taking their prize home. This obstacle is rooted in their own worst fears and toxic narratives of the past. It might take the shape of a villain or adversary. And then our hero fails. They lose, and they plunge into the pit of despair. The dreams and hopes that were so close to being realised are crushed. The girl has gone off with someone else, or has already left town or has just flat-out said no. This is the 'all is lost' moment, or the 'dark night of the soul'. In many stories and films, this moment is linked to a loss. The hero wonders how things can ever be right again. The journey seems wasted, and all the wins and revelations count for nothing. Act 2 ends when out of the fog of failure our hero comes up with a plan, an idea, an inspiration. This inspiration could only happen when all the old stories and ways of thinking have failed. Under the weight of disaster, the original DNA, the deep heart of the hero, rises up to save the day.

Are you in Act 2?

If so, are you:

- Starting out on the journey into the unknown with a few key allies?

- At a point of surrender, revelation and deeper understanding?

- At the 'all is lost' moment?

- Having a new idea that might just work?

A core part of any personal change involves facing the conflicts that we have with others, but the greater conflict we must face is the one we have with ourselves, our shadow. A great example is Christopher Nolan's take on the Batman franchise, which shows how the Joker is a character who embodies Batman's inner darkness and chaos.[5] In many stories, the hero's own dark aspects might be projected onto the villain or antagonist, but eventually, usually in their 'all is lost' moment, the hero must face and deal with their own fear, lust, hate or sadness. Doing so moves them from conflict into reconciliation and integration. Story can give us a route map through our own conflicts.

---

5   C Nolan, *The Dark Knight* (Warner Bros., 2008)

Act 3

Act 3 often starts with our hero standing in the power of their new story and authentic self. They are wiser, maybe humbler, and ready to finally take home the prize. This is the ultimate showdown with their nemesis/shadow/greatest fear/old story. It's where Harry Potter has his showdown with Voldermort.[6] This is also the moment when the truth of our hero is finally made visible to the world. Now there's no doubt. Cinderella is revealed as the princess she always was. It's also the moment when our hero takes decisive action and strikes the killer blow to achieve both the internal and external goal. It's the moment where the new story and role that has been developing all along finally kicks in, and we see that the hero is changed forever.

After their win, the hero starts to make their way home. But home is no longer the same as when they left it because they've changed. Home will need to change to accommodate the hero's growth and change. In this final act, we might get a glimpse of the hero's reconfigured life. In romcoms, this is where we get a hint of the new relationship to come in the last reel kiss.

These three acts comprise a descent from the known world into the unknown shadows and a return to

---

6   D Yates, *Harry Potter and the Deathly Hallows* (Warner Bros., 2011)

the known world with a new perspective and way of being. To me as a life coach and psychotherapist, this has strong parallels with the journey a client might make through the process of coaching or therapy. They often start therapy in response to a triggering event, which could simply be a new realisation that they don't know how to process. The old story and the old role have fallen apart under the weight of a new situation. They need to develop better stories and roles. This usually means a certain amount of deconstruction of old, previously-taken-for-granted narratives. The 'new self' or 'new story' that emerges through therapy could be described as more flexible, compassionate and inclusive rather than entirely new. This motif of sinking into darkness as a route to enlightenment is also a strong narrative within religions and mystic practices.

Pursuing the prize

A story is a sequence of events driven by a character in pursuit of an objective. The character could be an individual or an organisation. Along the way, our hero must face obstacles that stand between their prize and them. Some of these blocks will be internal – fear and insecurity, for example. These are rooted in an aspect of our hero's past story and experience. Other blocks are external – economic conditions and competitors, for example. How they manage to overcome these obstacles will reveal not only the person they are, but also the person they are becoming. By the end of the story, they will have both reached their objective (outer goal, eg get the girl/boy) and faced and worked through an internal obstacle (inner goal eg overcome fear of rejection).

The reader or audience identifies emotionally with the characters as well as the unfolding plot and the dilemmas that drive decisions along the way. The hero faces dilemmas every time they reach an obstacle, and often these are dilemmas we can all identify with. Many of my clients have these dilemmas. I remember working with Joe, a young man with an addiction to alcohol. His dilemma was whether to go forward into an unknown but sober future or stay with the familiar and comfortable method of coping with the bottle. These dilemmas, conflicts and obstacles often escalate over the course of a story, until the hero eventually feels overwhelmed by the pressure. This is the 'dark night of the soul' moment. In classic storytelling, the big breakthrough, the sudden realisation of a solution or a great idea or a plan to defeat the enemy, will come out of it. This moment is followed by a breakthrough into new power and ability, which propels the hero into achieving their inner and outer objectives.

Plot

Plot is the sequence of actions and reactions that runs from start to finish in a story. Each action is usually caused by the previous one and is a result of reaching toward the goals just described. The plot of any story, including our own, is a series of turning points. For better or worse, these are the actions that we take through life. They are all our decisions strung together like pearls. Each pearl is an experience characterised by change.

Plot is a sequence of happenings that drive the story forward. It's not about feelings or moods or thoughts per se. It's about actions. These actions are an expression of our stories, but depending on how they go, they might also lead us to create new stories. Without a plot there is no story. In the UK, there used to be a show called *This Is Your Life*. The presenter would whisk celebrities off to a studio, where the plot points of their lives would be retold. Both the highs and the lows were revealed.

You can find the plot in your life by creating a timeline of plot points. These will be points in your life when a) an event happened and b) you reacted to it in some way. Some reactions are a result of trying to avoid change, and some are born of the desire to do something different. Those in the second category are plot points that will have moved your story forward. You might be surprised by the results of this exercise. Are there as many plot points as you expected, or have you generally played safe and tried to hold on to the familiar story? In other words, did you jump or stick?

EXERCISE: Plot your timeline

1. Draw a timeline as a straight line from birth to your current age.

2. Drop into the timeline six turning-point events for you. Don't think about it too hard – write down the first that come to mind. They can be from any time in your life.

3. Alongside each event, write a sentence in response to these questions:

   – How did the event make you feel?

   – How did you react – did you jump or stick?

   When you step back and look at these plot points, do you see a theme or an overall story emerge?

Sometimes this exercise reveals recurring patterns. It's not unusual to react to different situations in a similar way.

The events in the plot can be painful or joyful, but they all drive our life story in a particular direction. Plot is about big and small decisions. It's about the forks in the road and the decisions we've taken. It's about the road we follow.

CASE STUDY – TERRIE

Terrie, a woman in her mid-thirties, came to see me because she kept having arguments with her partner,

Lucy. Sometimes these fights bordered on physical. Something needed to change and quick if Terrie was to escape this cycle of anger and remorse. We did the timeline exercise, and it became clear that she had a recurring theme of being let down by people. Her parents split up when she was six, and then she ended up being looked after by an aunt whom she idolised. Unfortunately, after a few years her aunt died, and Terrie entered into a cycle of foster homes. It seemed that no one could stay on the pedestal she placed them on, and when they inevitably fell off their plinth, Terrie would be overcome with rage and disappointment. It seemed that a recurring plot point on her timeline was a dramatic relationship breakdown. Once Terrie saw the plot line of her life, she started approaching her relationship in a more tolerant and forgiving way.

Structure and repetition

When I was a child, I loved playing games based on characters I'd seen in my favourite TV shows. Like most kids, I had an inherent sense of the game's rules, boundaries and parameters. If these weren't adhered to, the game would fall apart. The rules enabled me to play.

We all need rules to help us know what to do in any given situation. Often these rules are unconscious and attached to old stories. But that doesn't make them any less powerful. Rules are a necessary and helpful part of life. Businesses would fold without shared and agreed rules for commerce. Stories only work according to the rules that act as internal scaffolding. Whatever our story is, it will lead us to believe that certain things must, should or ought to be done. If you grew up thinking people from other countries 'come over here and steal our jobs', then you may be more likely to agree with any rule that says, 'We must keep those people out'. We can also make rules in reaction to our experience of others. If someone has been mistreated by men, it wouldn't be surprising if they developed a fairly negative story about men. This could lead to the rule that says, 'Never trust any man'. In these cases, the rules are rooted in painful experience and can be quite limiting.

Story provides an organising structure and pattern to our lives. This is one of the most appealing aspects of story – it forms shapes out of the background chaos. Growing up, I was confused about who I was, what the point of life was and what would make life meaningful. Stories gave me a structure to hang my life upon. A big part of structure is repetition and predictable order. Children's stories often have a high degree of this. It creates a safe container around new ideas and experiences. People often think of creative activities such as acting and storytelling as free-flowing, spontaneous and maybe even wild. But as any professional artist knows, there must be order and structure or nothing will happen. Professional writers, when asked about their process, will often say it's less about inspiration and more about turning up every day and doing the work between set times that never change. One of my guests on my *Pivot Points* podcast was the actress

Tamzin Merchant. She's written a popular book for young people and described the importance of sticking to set times for writing whether she felt like it or not.[7] We need structure and boundaries to create safety and predictability. This is important for life as much as for art.

Final thoughts

What is your structure like? Could you build up more structure and repetition in your life? It might be helpful to return to the three-act structure.

In this chapter we have looked at the importance of structure. In many stories this can be seen in a three-act structure. The plotline of stories and indeed our own lives is usually a series of actions in pursuit of something: a prize. While this prize may be tangible, for example financial success, it is also a pursuit of deeper needs, for example self-worth or love. Structure means that one thing builds on another to produce a result. If there is no structure your story can lose power, get confused and fall back into repetitive and unproductive habits. So, although structure is often seen as in opposition to life and creativity it is actually essential to human flourishing.

---

7   A Radmall, 'Creativity and writing (with Tamzin Merchant)', *Pivot Points* (2020), www.pivotpointspodcast.co.uk/creativity-and-writing-with-tamzin-merchant, accessed 12 May 2021

TWO

Colouring In The Outline

W e've looked at how a story is constructed. Now we'll put some flesh on the bones and start to colour in the outline of what creates a narrative.

Zoom in, zoom out

Story is an exercise in editing. When we tell each other stories about our lives, we leave lots of stuff out. This is because a story has one core theme, one key point that it's driving toward. The architecture of story helps us step back from the chaos of everyday reality and foreground particular aspects of life's white noise. It's this very distancing function of story that paradoxically enables us to enter it in such an immersive way.

In fictional stories, aesthetic distance is the knowledge that whatever happens is 'just a story', 'not real' or 'make-believe'. This separation between our 'real' lives and the story frees us up to jump into the story as observer and from the POV (point of view) of the characters. The mirror neurons in our brain allow us to go beyond observation and into empathising with the characters. Without this empathy, we wouldn't enter stories or be so moved by them. The power of story is that our brains make almost no distinction between what's happening to the character and what's happening to us.

This is a key that unlocks much of this book.

Our feelings, bodies, minds and hearts will follow what our imagination tells us. The imagination trumps the rational mind most times. Our brains don't distinguish between whether the person we're watching is our mother (real life) or a character in a movie (fictional life). The power of theatre, cinema and novels pulls us into the pages, the screen and the hearts of the characters. We identify with what they feel, want what they want and become massively invested in their success. The paradox is that because we know it's make-believe, we relax and allow ourselves to become immersed. As a therapist, I'm in the business of helping people step back from their experiences enough for them to see that it's just one possible story. Equally, I'm working with people to help them enter new stories and roles that they feel in their core and have almost no distance from. I call it zooming in and zooming out.

Once we're able to see our life as a story, we can step back from it. This often means zooming out of our rational, empirical mind and into an alternative POV. From this zoomed-out POV, we start to see that whatever story we've been focusing on is just one possible iteration out of an infinite number of possible narratives. This position is often linked to a less dualistic and more spiritual perspective. It's from and with this POV that we can more easily zoom in on an aspect of life and re-narrate it. It's also easier to visualise, dream and imagine from a zoomed-out position. This isn't a disembodied state. Being zoomed out doesn't mean we're disconnected from our bodies and breath. Quite the reverse – this tends to happen more when we're zoomed in.

Story and shadow

The best stories refract the many facets of humanity like diamonds refract light. They allow us to engage with both the hero and villain inside our own hearts. All the way back to the Greek theatre, story and drama has enabled us to face the horrors and shadows lurking in the soul. In doing this, story has the unique ability to connect mind, heart, body and soul and allow us to process things the mind would usually defend itself against. The words, symbols, plots and roles within story act as a bridge between our hearts and minds. Story creates integration and communication.

We all have parts of ourselves, experiences or feelings we try to either bury or compartmentalise. These are often at odds with how we'd like to see ourselves. Story helps us to face these shadows and work through them via the narrative. In most stories, the obstacles the hero has to work through are actually parts of themselves that they've never come to terms with. A lot of the work in analytic psychotherapy is in reintegrating our shadow with our conscious awareness. This can be facilitated by moving into the more magical and dreamlike landscape provided by imagination, story and creativity. Although I won't focus on the idea of shadow in this book, we'll look at the importance of facing shadows when it comes to growing and breaking free of old stories. The shadow may appear to us as a nemesis or a fear, and yet, once faced and integrated, it can become the pivot into a more empowered life story.

The best stories, particularly fairy tales and mythic tales, aren't dualistic. They embrace the shadow aspects of humanity. Greek myths put us face to face with the most extreme aspects of our subconscious and enable us to metabolise those shadows. In Ancient Greece, people watched tragedy to view their own ghastly impulses around rage, lust and insanity. But the aesthetic distance between stage and audience provided a safe container for the pain.

Society has always used story, whether in the form of comedy or tragedy, to hold a mirror up to itself, to see itself more clearly and work through its complex issues. Fairy tales contain the shadows of the unconscious and even help children face and work through their terrors. The fact that it's only a story makes it safe for us to face our shadow in it.

Story and identity

Our identity is deeply interwoven with our story. When you share your story with someone else, you also share your identity. By identity, I mean the role you play in everyday life – the persona that is 'played out' in relationships with others. Depending on the type of relationship we're in, our identity and role will shift and change. You could say that we're most ourselves when interacting with others in the ongoing play of life. We all need an audience if we're to tell our story. Hopefully the audience cheers us on. We know that a child is more likely to thrive when they're encouraged and loved. This strengthens a resilient identity.

Our identity is the expression of our story, but it isn't fixed – it's quite responsive to our situation and context. Later in this book, we'll go deeper into the tools for transforming our identity as well as our underlying narrative.

Everyone is a performer. Everyone is playing at least one role in at least one story. The line between fiction and non-fiction is a blur. I believe that even 'real' stories are constructed and fictional. Just because stories are created in response to life events doesn't mean that they're not also edited, shaped and yes, even fiction-alised. I don't mean to belittle the stories I've heard as a therapist. They may be gut-wrenchingly hard and full of genuine pain and trauma. But unless we can acknowledge that to some extent these stories are narrated, curated and edited by us, we stand no chance of changing them and writing a better story to live.

Over the years, I've learned to look for a particular pivot point in my clients. It's that moment when they realise that what they'd always thought was the *indisputable truth* is actually a narrative. Once they realise this, they simultaneously wake up to the fact that if this is a story, then it's only one way of seeing life. That means there could be alternative stories, better stories, kinder and more energising stories. This moment is deep. The person wakes up to the reality that they might not be who they thought they were – because stories define identity. This means that if a story shifts, so does someone's identity. This is as true in business as it is for individuals. If a business wants to change, it needs to first understand the story it's intentionally or unintentionally been telling its customers about what it is.

This book will show you ways to see the stories you're already telling, to emphasise your role as narrator and then to use the skills of acting to build and enact a new story.

EXERCISES: What's your story?

Your story as a film

If your story were a film, what genre would it be? A thriller, a romance, a comedy or a horror? If you're not sure, ask a few friends. Then imagine a film is being made of your life. Which actor or character could play the role of you?

The answers to these questions will start to reveal the kind of story you're living in the world.

Now imagine that people who know you are being interviewed about you, like in a documentary. What do you think they would say?

- What would they say are your most and least appealing traits?
- What would they miss most about you if you weren't around?
- What wouldn't they miss if you weren't around?

Once you've gathered this information, consider if this is the kind of story you want to be putting out into the world. Many of my clients find it a shock to discover what kind of story they're telling or others are telling about them. This process can be the first step to changing your life story.

Timeline

Some people find it helpful to draw a timeline with the key events of their lives marked on it, similar to the exercise in Chapter 1. You could use images or words to mark key points. Whether the events are positive or negative, they're plot points in that they mark shifts and changes in your life. Now ask yourself what conclusion or story you might have told yourself about each of these events. Do you start to see a theme or an overarching narrative appearing? What do you think about this story?

Drawing a map

Consider these questions.

- If you were at a party and someone said, 'Tell me about yourself,' what would you say? What would you leave out of this story?

- What events in your past have had the most influence over who you are now?

- What do you value in a person above all else?

- In terms of your actions, what are your musts, shoulds and oughts? How much or how little do you fulfil these?

- Which three fictional characters might be considered the opposite of who you are? Which three might be considered similar to you?

Now complete these sentences:

- The world is…
- People are…
- I am…

You've just drawn a map of your 'regular story' – the one that's told and untold, visible and invisible – its values, beliefs, influences and limitations. You've increased your mindfulness about your old narratives. Now consider that this story is just one of many possible truths about who you are. New stories could be told that allow for greater freedom and creativity.

Final thoughts

There's an undiscovered world beyond our current stories that we know nothing about. Yet. Our life story is a small piece of a much bigger pie. Beyond that slice is huge potential.

Becoming more flexible about how we enact and tell our story frees us up to move between roles, situations and relationships while still maintaining an authentic sense of self.

THREE

How To Make A Life Story

In this chapter we will look at the different kinds of stories that can end up as a life script. These stories come from our origins, culture and family. We are largely unaware of these stories and yet they form the scripts for how we live our lives.

Origin stories

The stories we're exposed to early in life tend to define who we think we are, what the world is like and how to relate to others. Stories act as a road map for living. Much of the time, we're using these maps without realising they're only maps. Stories from our early life, family, culture, TV, film and books can all feed into a big melting pot called *the incontrovertible truth*.

Although stories shape us, we're often unaware of how much of our 'true' story about the world, others and ourselves is actually dependent on our family and culture of origin. Consider how many politicians shout into the echo chamber of their own culture's *incontrovertible truth*. This dependency doesn't make our narratives wrong, but it does make them partial at best. In my experience as a therapist and coach, I constantly help clients whose biggest problem is that they don't realise that they're living out stories about life and themselves that they've inherited from others. These stories are like invisible cages that keep them stuck.

I remember working in a mental-health day centre. I'd been there a couple of days when a middle-aged man approached me. The first words he said were, 'Hi, I'm Reg, and I'm a manic depressive and take fifty milligrams of anti-psychotics to take the edge off my symptoms.' I was struck by how this man told me his identity story in one sentence. But don't we do this when we introduce ourselves to others socially? We carry these highly edited and limited stories around with us, ready to perform at a moment's notice.

We'll never be able to break out of our narrative prison unless we understand the nature of our origin story. This is true for both businesses and individuals.

So what exactly is an origin story?

In all cultures, there are big explanatory and cosmological stories that tell us why we're here and what life is about. These could be religious and enacted in ritual and forms of worship. Anthropology shows that these cosmological stories are often invoked at points of life transition. Rites of passage such as marriage, death, birth and becoming an adult all refer to the bigger, explanatory story. And that's because it's at these points, liminal stages of transition, that we most need to be anchored in the explanatory metanarrative.

There are also secular versions of the cosmological story in science and psychology. Quantum physics has highlighted how all life at the subatomic level is chaos, energy and uncertainty. One of the functions of explanatory stories is to bring order out of the chaos, to explain that life has some kind of purpose and meaning. Many stories reinforce this with good-vs-bad narratives. Good is linked to order and bad is linked to disorder, rebellion, selfishness and chaos. I think of story as a way in which we organise the alphabet soup of life into meaningful forms of living.

Each of us has a unique origin story. It's formed by the way life events and stories of family, culture, religion and geographical location bounce off each other. An origin story will complete any sentence that starts with 'I'm like this because...' Events happen to us, good and bad, and then we filter our understanding of these events through a mixture of feelings and the available narratives in whatever context we live in. These stories can quickly harden into beliefs that take on the rock-solid certainty of truth. We then proceed to view life through the filter of these stories.

Origin stories are present in personal and business life. I once coached a company that had lost a key client because of poor communication. This happened early in their start-up phase. The company became convinced that they were poor at comms, so they drafted in an expensive comms team. When I worked with them, it became clear they were good at communication – they just needed to learn some basic storytelling skills.

CASE STUDY – ALEXANDRIA

Alexandria, an ex-model who'd become a famous actress, was used to being in demand, adored and talked about. She seemed to have everything: money, beauty and fame. When I first started working with her, she was almost unable to leave her house and full of self-hatred. She had an origin story of being abused as a child and had been told by her mother all her life that she was a slut and men only wanted her for one thing. She had a strong narrative that told her to be ashamed of being seen and admired. The first thing Alexandria had to do was understand that this story wasn't reality but something she'd been given by her mother and had been wearing ever since, like an overcoat. Once she saw there might be other stories she could live, her self-hatred and fear lessened and she was able to enjoy parts of her life she was previously ashamed of.

Stories *are* identity – they tell us who we are and how we should behave. There seems to be an innate need in us to hold on to the story of our identity no matter how fragmented or damaged it might be. Any identity is better than none.

Our stories about who we are will generally operate below the level of consciousness but assume the mantle of unquestionable truth. We cannot change the stories we're living unless we understand what they are. To do this, we need to think about how stories are made. It can be shocking to discover that what we thought and assumed was 'normal' was based simply on reactions to specific and circumstantial experiences.

Origin stories contain the DNA of the authentic you, however 'bad' or 'toxic' they are – you can track your deep calling and mission in the world at different points in your origin narrative. There are moments when the authentic self pops out from behind the dominant story. These moments may be in the context of school, family or friendships. I remember stepping up to read from the Bible in front of a church when I was seven. I realised I loved being in front of a crowd with a text – yet in every other part of life I was painfully shy and hid away from the world. In that one moment I discovered something that was waiting to be seen and has become an increasingly realised part of my life: I'm an actor, a performer, a speaker.

EXERCISE: Uncovering the true story

Think about the moments when you felt most alive and engaged as a child. These may well have contradicted the dominant narrative of your origin story. Make a list of these moments. See what friends and family can tell you about when you acted 'out of character'.

It's likely that these moments were glimpses of your authentic story pushing through into everyday life. Rather like Cinderella at the ball – the princess within had to come out sooner or later, no matter how hard others tried to suppress it. The true story is often hiding in plain sight inside our dominant origin story.

We construct explanatory stories out of past experiences and our reactions to them. The fact that those experiences and reactions are no longer happening doesn't stop us from wheeling them out on a regular basis. We all use the grid of past story to make sense of the present. Unfortunately, this often skews and distorts how we understand what's going on.

Culture stories

We're also shaped by invisible forces in the culture around us. These include the unspoken and sometimes spoken rules about gender, sexuality, class, geography, religion, ethnicity, race and economics. These rules are like different threads of a web that forms around and through us. Without thinking about it, we're hugely influenced by others' stories – those of our family, faith groups and culture. These all tell us who we are and are often supercharged with a moral force that tells us what we should do and how we should perform. No one is an island, and no one starts from a neutral position. These stories may or may not be toxic, but they're the currents and forces that shape our identity.

In terms of how we form our story about ourselves, education looms large. Unfortunately, it can be deeply scarring and shaming. I certainly remember some aspects of my school life that weren't designed to make me grow in self-acceptance and confidence – for example, the times my maths teacher would throw a blackboard eraser above my head in frustration. We also pick up stories about how life is and who we are in the scheme of things from faith traditions and assumptions about class and gender. These are never neutral stories. They're loaded with moral imperatives, such as 'men must be strong', 'people with money are always exploitative' or 'never trust someone who is this colour'.

I grew up in a white middle-class family near the sea. I never interacted with people from other cultures, who were from different races or who had sexual orientations that were different from mine. I was taken to church and developed an idea of God based on fear and distance. I learned about sex from porn, and my primary relationships were with my toy soldiers and shows on TV. I wanted to live inside the glamour on display in many shows from the seventies. I watch these shows now and shudder.

This network, or web, undoubtedly shaped not only my sense of who I was but also my story about what the world was like.

Family stories

The events, traumas and joys that impact us as we grow up usually originate from within family relationships. By *family*, I refer to the network of people you're most in contact with during your early life. Early experiences, good or bad, become the foundation of a life story. They're woven into the network of the relationships around us as we grow up.

The biggest event that impacted me was the trauma of being separated from my mother at birth. The existential horror of being adopted as a baby was compounded by a failure to attach to my parents as I grew up. Not surprisingly, this led to a background feeling of being alone and disconnected from others.

Also in my early life, our family home was surrounded by several mental-health hospitals. My parents were so afraid that I might be attacked by one of the 'lunatics' that they barred me from playing outside the house.

This impacted my already fragile attempts to make friends with other kids.

For many years, I chose to tell my family story from the perspective of deficit and loss. I could have told another story, though – one of gratitude that I wasn't taken into care. If I had, I would almost certainly have ended up in a children's home in Jersey that later became notorious as a place of systematic abuse.

The foundations of our identity are to some extent formed in our relationships with others and the world around us. The way our primary caregivers react to us can easily become the way we react to ourselves. So if we grew up with acceptance and love, this is likely to be the approach we take with ourselves as we mature. I have more than one friend who was told while growing up with loving parents that they were loved, that they were kings or queens and that they would make a big impression on the world. And they did! One is now a successful screen actor.

We can react to relationships in two ways: retreat or embrace. This leads us to another key aspect of how our story gets formed. Just because two people have experienced similar trauma in their early life doesn't mean they'll have the same challenges in later life. It's how we react to these experiences that makes all the difference.

Sometimes when I teach people how identity narratives are formed, I draw a picture of a flower with many petals. At the heart of the flower is the identity. The petals represent the different forces that shape and influence a person's narrative. These petals include not only traumas but also the stories we tell ourselves and that other people tell about us. I remember once overhearing my mother complaining about me to a friend. She was saying how irresponsible I was and what a worry I was to her. This confirmed my (probably incorrect) suspicion that she really didn't like me. It also reinforced my growing suspicion that I was 'trouble'.

These stories aren't just influential: they carry the weight of truth and certainty. They're never simply abstract, disembodied theories. They're never simply conceptual. They're usually imprinted on us physically. We experience these stories on both an emotional and physical level. When others' narratives cross our psychic/physical boundaries in an aggressive, violent, sexualised or neglectful way, trauma imprints can happen. This kind of physicalised storytelling is hardwired into us at the neurological and physical level.

We all need to operate from a position of certainty, and these stories enable us to do that. It's important to see this because it seems that much therapy and self-help focuses too heavily on rearranging the conceptual furniture and ignores the need for the body to recode and retell these narratives. This only happens through physical action. As we'll explore, the most effective way to do this is via acting techniques.

Our lived experiences culminate in stories that link to core beliefs about ourselves and others. These core stories act as pegs on which to hang the way we see ourselves and the world around us. In my life, I developed a core story that said I was a reject and that unless I made others like me, I'd be rejected again. Core stories can be positive or negative. Not only are they based on emotional reactions to experiences, but they also trigger emotions. As a teenager, I believed that one wrong step and I'd be rejected by my friends. This led to a background feeling of anxiety and fear.

As well as emotions, these core stories told also lead to a moral framework by which we live: the shoulds, oughts and musts that govern our actions in the world – as we've discussed, the rules. My core story of rejection keyed into a moral imperative: I *must* make others happy with me or else they'll reject me. How I reacted to this moral order and told story led me into my lived story.

As human beings, we're dependent on core stories because the alternative is to sink into the chaos. Occasionally this happens anyway, particularly in times of trauma, change or loss. Much of my work as a coach and therapist involves helping people find and construct stories that will act as ladders out of the chaos and disorientation of trauma. Without story, it's almost impossible to make sense of life or know how to precede. Again, stories aren't just a list of rules, ideas or concepts. They're maps for living.

Stories are like a grid that we place over our experiences to tell us how to make sense of them. Often we select and focus on experiences that fit with our explanatory model. I grew up on the lookout for any sign that I was being rejected because I'd developed a story about rejection based on my emotional experience. So I saw rejection but often missed the love and acceptance that was also all around me.

Along with helping us to understand what's going on, stories help us take a moral position regarding what's happening. Is it good, bad, irrelevant? Should we be responding and moving into action? If so, what action should we be taking?

This grid is often based on the answers to these questions:

1. The world is...

2. People are...

3. I am...

4. I must always...

5. I must never....

The answers to a), b) and c) tend to lead to the answers to d) and e).

CASE STUDY - BOB

Two men were talking in an office. One was the company's CEO. The other was Bob's ambitious colleague Tom. Bob had a longstanding narrative that Tom was after his job. This caused him a lot of stress.

He noticed Tom and the CEO laughing and occasionally looking over at him. Later that day, Bob asked Tom what he'd been talking about with the CEO. Tom just winked and said, 'Wait and see.' This sent Bob into full panic mode.

That evening, just as Bob was getting ready to go home, Tom sidled up to him and said, 'The boss wants to see you in the conference room.'

As Bob opened the door to the room, he was already writing his résumé for another job. But when he looked up, he saw that the conference room was packed with colleagues, family and friends. The CEO stepped forward, slapped him on the back and wished him a happy birthday. Then Tom came forward with a gift package. Inside was the watch Bob had told Tom weeks ago that he wanted. That afternoon, the CEO and Tom had finalised where they were going to buy the present for their esteemed colleague.

People create stories like Bob's all the time. How often have you come up with a story that does explain what you're experiencing in a coherent way but isn't actually the correct explanation? In this book, we'll be looking a lot at how stories organise the complex flow of data running through our lives from moment to moment. How we experience life depends on whether these stories are toxic or healthy. If toxic, like Bob's, then anxiety and fear will continually be triggered in us. These stories are also narrow and fixed. They're full of moral imperatives such as 'this is the way it has to be or really is' and 'there's no other explanation'. By contrast, healthy stories are more flexible and able to accommodate different circumstances. Viewing life through the lens of healthy stories will lead to greater energy, optimism and hopefulness.

Enacted stories

The enacted story is the surface story that we live out in daily life. It's the tip of the iceberg that's visible and in our awareness. It's our persona. Of course, we play different roles depending on the relationship we're engaged in at any given moment. I play several roles – therapist, teacher, actor and consultant – and I express myself quite differently in each one. What we're usually quite unaware of is how powerfully our life stories are driving us in the day-to-day. My story of rejection and needing to please or impress people led me to living a story where I either entertain people (on stage) or make them feel better. While there's integrity and value in these things, an element of me living out my story led me to them in the first place.

The stories we tell are inextricably linked to the roles we play. The roles reinforce the stories and vice versa. The more we put our stories into action, the more real they seem to be. This is why we cannot just change the story; we must also work on the roles embedded inside our stories. This goes further than therapy that remains at the level of talking but not acting.

Who is the author?

All of this raises a key question: who is the author of our life stories? We often assume we are. But there's the massive influence of our past experiences and how we react to them to consider. This includes the influence of culture, faith traditions, gender stories and economic opportunities. So who's writing your story?

This book is about putting power back into your hands, so you can be the author of your story going forward. Of course, as mentioned, no one is an island, so when it comes to re-authoring your life or business story, it will be important to collaborate with family, partners, friends and colleagues. The point here is that you're not doomed to continually live out old stories.

You are not your past life. And anyone can change.

Behind every story is an author. Who's the author of the story you're living right now? Is it you? God? Other people? Your past?

Whether we're seeking others' approval or rehashing what our parents told us, we're frequently not the authors of our own story. As a Christian, I used to think that God was the author of my story. The Christian tradition I was raised in focused on how we could put ourselves to death so that the spiritual life of God could take over. And it seemed to make sense that God was the author of everything. But now I believe that God may be a co-author in a process that's our responsibility. This is also one of the big shifts that happens in a story, whether it's in a novel, a film or a therapy session. The hero starts to take responsibility for writing their own story, or perhaps co-writing it.

I'm not suggesting taking an ego-driven, selfish, me-first approach that involves getting others to dance to your tune. That's nothing short of narcissism. I'm suggesting taking responsibility for your story by showing up and taking part in others' lives. But there should be give and take with the people you engage with. Their stories should not control you, nor should you seek to control them. This kind of interaction underpins all healthy relationships.

What if the story that is co-authored exists in the space between people? What if there's a sense of taking responsibility for authoring one's own story as well as entering a pre-existing narrative? Actors must leave behind the narratives that life has imprinted on them to shift into a narrative that fits the story, the play, the film.

I once attended a workshop that utilised dramatic narratives and characters from plays to enable participants to leave behind old narratives. It didn't lead to me simply recycling my old stories, or to me passively allowing an author's narrative to shape me. Instead, I acted as a co-author in the space between my old narrative and the fictional one that raised me into that co-authored space.

Final thoughts

It's empowering to consider that we're co-authors of our life story. This idea can help us move away from the sense that we're trapped inside stories beyond our control. In the book *Room*, the two central characters, a mother and her young son, are trapped in a small room. The boy makes up stories and characters out of the objects and fittings of the space. This gives him some sense of ownership and authorship. And yet, someone else has established the parameters of his world.[8]

We're like this boy when we tell stories in reaction to our circumstances. But we can take ownership. We can tell new stories outside the random room of our personal circumstances.

---

8   E Donoghue, *Room* (Picador, 2011)

FOUR

Good Story Vs Bad Story

There's a big difference between toxic, destructive stories that drain us of life and healthy, life-giving narratives. Many of the clients I see have been living their whole lives in a bad story that they never question. But as we've discussed, a story is just one possible framing of events that could be replaced with a new one. If you're living out a bad story, don't you think it's time to wake up, smell the roses and make a change?

Are you living in a bad story or a good one? What criteria would you use to tell the difference? Let's explore this.

Bad stories

In my work with families, couples, individuals and organisations over the years, I've come to understand the power of bad stories. People can so easily define themselves and become imprisoned by them.

CASE STUDY – EVIE

The teenage daughter, Evie, of a family I worked with was seen by the rest of the family as *the problem* because she wouldn't eat. Her anorexia was an affront to how they saw themselves – as a caring family. So rather than look at their own disharmony, anger and unexpressed pain, they scapegoated Evie. They created a story that Evie found difficult to escape.

It's scary how often we can find ourselves living out stories that others have put on us. These negative narratives quickly become agreed 'truth'. It took some time, but through therapy we were able to look at some better stories – ones that allowed Evie to contribute and not just be seen as 'bad'. As we changed the negative story to a positive one, Evie's behaviour began changing for the better. We started this process by identifying a moment in which Evie was seen as more of a solution than a problem. In this case, it was when she suggested the family visit the zoo. This was out of character with the kind of behaviour the family usually focused on. More than that, it also demonstrated she had thought carefully about an activity everyone would enjoy.

The journey out of a negative story often starts when we identify a positive action that contradicts the negative narrative.

There are several key elements that to a greater or lesser degree will be present in all bad stories.

Fear of change

Bad stories tend to keep us stuck in the past. Instead of embracing new things as an opportunity to grow and transform, we'll shrink back, cling to how things used to be and swim with all our might back to the land of the familiar and known. In bad stories, there's fear of the new and unknown.

I had a client, let's call her Eddie, who couldn't let go of her mother, who'd passed away. She had a story about being a loyal helper to her mother. This blocked her from starting any new relationships and kept her grounded in the same life she lived as a teenager. She kept her mother's room frozen in time, like a shrine, full of photos, mementos and clothes that would never be worn again. Sometimes she'd even speak to her mother, whom she felt was constantly with her.

Although this was all part of the grief process, Eddie got stuck in it. It went on for months and then years. She refused many offers of dates and relationships. Her life got even smaller. By the time Eddie came to see me, she was ready to start the long journey back into a bigger life. But she was terrified of facing the rage and grief that had held her prisoner. There would never be any movement into a new life unless Eddie let go of the old story and made space for the new.

This isn't an easy pivot. In the early stages of breaking free, there can even be nostalgia for the 'way things used to be', however bad they were.

After a few months of work in therapy, Eddie joined a local social club, made some friends and started to build real friendships.

Bad stories are individualistic and ego-driven. Unfortunately, this fits with the way we perceive heroes in stories of success. The story about having to fight one's way to the top isn't only stressful – it also makes co-operation with others more difficult. Western culture can perpetuate the 'I did it my way' approach to life. This tends to close people down into a way of living which I call monologic (as opposed to dialogic).

Monologues

I first identified monologues in some research I was doing regarding clients with eating disorders. People stuck in monologues have only one perspective and aren't open to other voices. They tend to go round in circles and find other people's points of view unsettling and even irritating.

CASE STUDY – MONICA

When I worked with Monica, a brilliant eighteen-year-old with anorexia, we identified a monologue story that went something like this:

I feel fat. I am fat. The only solution is to lose weight. How can I lose weight? Now I've lost weight. But...I feel fat. I am fat. The only solution is to lose weight. How can I lose weight?

These monologues tend to go round and round in circles that never change. In this case, the decrease could be measured on the scales and by the alarming feeling that Monica was disappearing in front of me.

Monologue stories have a dreamy, unreal quality to them. The same story, the same POV, is repeated, over and over again, and no other story can be heard. We'd hate any novel or film that did this. It would be like watching paint dry. Of course, Monica's story is an extreme example. You may want to check with your friends. Do they hear you repeating similar stories, explanations and points of view?

Criticism and judgement

Bad stories shut people down. They stop them from considering other possible ways of seeing the world. This is usually linked to a tendency to be critical and judgemental toward others. There's little empathy for other points of view. In fact, these are often rubbished. There's a feeling that things must, should and ought to be done in this way and any deviation from that is wrong. Behind this lies a sense of shame, and the same level of judgement and criticism is also aimed at oneself if there's any perceived failure. People living these stories can be perfectionistic and intolerant. Bad stories seek out echo chambers. Anyone who opposes the story is perceived as wrong and bad. We tend to see this in politics, religion and social media. There's a high level of shame, fear and low self-esteem in the judgemental person.

Isolation

Bad stories usually cut us off from other people. They tell us we're not worthy of being heard, that if we try something we'll fail, that the safest thing to do is play small and hide our true nature from the world.

CASE STUDY - SUE

Sue, a woman in her late fifties, was living in a bad story that cut her off from the world. After her husband left her for another woman, she retreated into her house and became terrified of going anywhere. She'd been quite attached to her husband, Alan, who by all accounts was a domineering and larger-than-life character. Sue told herself she didn't have the confidence to do anything on her own, so she retreated behind her four walls.

This case highlighted the importance of taking action. It didn't matter how much I tried to convince her that she could change her story – it was only when she started to physically step out of her house that the story changed. First, she went to her front gate, then to the postbox, then to the shops and then round the park. It was only then, when there was physical evidence to back up a new story, that Sue changed her bad story and broke out of isolation.

Shame

Bad stories are often rooted in a sense of shame. If you feel guilty, you feel remorse for something you've done. If you feel shame, you feel bad about being who you are. People who have been shamed as children often have a deep narrative about being fundamentally bad or unlovable. People with shame often say things such as, 'If people really knew what I was like, they wouldn't want to know me.' Shame narratives are often interwoven with a sense of lacking the basic requirements to be accepted by others. So people with shame often become people-pleasers, hoping desperately that the more they fix, help, entertain or serve others, the more they'll be accepted. But the shame narrative is like corrosive acid to the soul, and until this story is faced and replaced, it will remain one of the biggest obstacles to transformation. Often people with shame will self-medicate with various addictions and activities that make them temporarily feel better.

Good stories

How to construct and live out good stories is at the heart of this book. We're all on a journey of pivoting from bad to good narratives. Before we get into the details of how to pivot, we need to understand the marks of a good story.

Dialogue

There's a moment when I know change has arrived for a client. It's the moment they're able to see a stuck situation from a new perspective. It's the moment they really consider another POV and break free of their stuck monologue. This is the essential ingredient of dialogue. Good stories have space in them to see things from other people's perspectives.

I recently spoke with a client who'd been stuck in a monologue for a long time. She told me that she'd been able to talk with her mother about their relationship and what was problematic in it. Why was this such a breakthrough? Because she'd shifted from a perspective where all she could see was her version of events to being able to see both points of view and talk about the whole relationship. This kind of perspective shift is a sure sign that a dialogue with new possibilities is opening up. Once this pivot happens, new stories can be told and lived. When two points of view emerge where before there was only one, you have a dialogue. You have options. Good stories have this element of choice.

This isn't possible under conditions of anxiety or trauma when a person retreats into self-defence and can see only their own feelings. The more relaxed and open to other perspectives a person is, the more chance a new story can be told. The hero can relate to others differently.

When I'm counselling couples, I know that change is coming when someone says something such as, 'I never knew you felt like that'. Good stories are the opposite of narcissistic. They flow into the world and make it a better place. They're all about making the world a better, fairer, more loving place. To this end, they're often about creating reconciliation, relationship and redemption between people and between individuals and their own hearts.

Head and heart

Whereas bad stories tend to get us stuck in our egos and heads, good ones move us into our hearts. This doesn't mean emotion takes over and rationality is lost. It means that rationality, a key part of story structure, is now supported by the heart rather than divorced from it. Good stories appeal to head and heart, to structure and emotion, to predictability and disruption. For a good story to be lived, there must be a balance of head and heart. Too much of either and the story gets chaotic or rigid. And then it's not really a story because the nature of all good stories is that they evolve and change.

Having said this, a key part of many stories is the building up of repetition and a clear sense of order in the plot and characters. Without this order in place, it's not possible for the heart to come online. Good stories engage both mind and heart because they are intrinsically non-dualistic.

Facing the shadow

Often in good stories there comes a point where the hero faces their demons. Their worst fears are often represented in the people whom they find most difficult, their antagonists. In my experience as a therapist I have found that health, balance and self-acceptance is restored when people step out from behind their defensive barricades and face the parts of themselves they feel least comfortable with. This could be described as embracing the shadow side of ourselves.

Stories are perfect for helping us do this. Stories can hold the shit and glory together in one narrative. Stories can express loss and trauma because they use metaphors and symbols, enabling us to face and dialogue with those parts of ourselves we'd usually disassociate from and avoid. The symbols and metaphors we find in stories act as gateways into our darkest narratives. We can even face what we fear the most because 'it isn't really real'. I've come to believe that as a culture, we do most of our therapy work in front of the TV or in the cinema. Story gives us a chance to integrate and dialogue with the parts of ourselves that we may feel shame over in everyday life.

Transformation

Every good story is a road map for transformation. In most fictional stories, regardless of medium, the central characters 'go on a journey'. This is sometimes described as their character arc. As an audience, we get to see the mechanics of change. The hero may or may not achieve their objective, but they won't be in the same place either internally or externally at the end of the story.

The exception to this is comedy, where often the hero, or anti-hero, never learns from their mistakes. Regardless of how many humiliating failures they have, they approach life the same way. Our hero may get pushed down, but in the next episode, they'll bounce right back up. But even when the hero ends up where they began, they might go on a journey during the story.

Flow

Ultimately, good stories lift us out of our self-defensive egos and into the flow of life, which includes relationships with others, our world and our environment. It's like stepping into a fast-flowing river. Living a good story gives us energy, movement and a certain amount of unpredictability. It's a way of living that's more improvised, which we'll look at later.

So, a good story is more than being free, more than self-actualisation, more than getting over our fears and showing up, more than engaging with our magical influence on the world. It's also about joining the cosmic dance that underpins all reality. This dance is between us and others, between us and divinity. This dance is flow.

Psychologists have written a lot about flow. It's hard to describe being 'in flow', but we know when we're in it. We're in flow when our ability is equal to the challenge and we're operating out of our true selves. My clients often report more of these moments of flow when their stories start to open up and get bigger.

When I was starting out as an actor, I'd spend hours preparing for every performance. I'd go through my lines. All of them. I'd go through all my actions and movements. I might do some vocal and physical warm-ups. By the time I hit the stage, I was a nervous wreck. My small story about having to please people (the

audience) or face my sense of worthlessness was running me like a wind-up toy. I wasn't in flow because
flow is unconscious competence. I was far too self-
aware for that.

This all changed one night after I read a book about
acting. The writer described switching off self-con-
sciousness and relaxing. I stopped all the obsessive
prep and surrendered to the process. I started listening
to my fellow actors, and then my responses came nat-
urally, without hesitation or thought. I felt as if I were
a relaxed part of everything happening in and around
me. I was no longer seeing the audience as 'them' but
'us'. My mind stepped back, allowing me to be in the
flow of the present moment – listening, responding,
being aware. I had moved from monologue to dialogue.
I had entered flow.

These moments of flow and dialogue are transcendent,
even spiritual. They take us outside the room of our
usual story and open us up to a world we were perhaps
only dimly aware of. Of course, these moments can
fade as quickly as they arise, but they are signposts of
a bigger story.

When we're stuck in the loops of recurring stories,
we're in a state of blocked energy. This can become
toxic. When we start to remove the blocks with the pro-
cesses described in this book, energy will automatically
flow. To be in flow is our natural state. So much of life
can feel like a dam that's made of fear. We know there's

a reservoir of water behind it, and we feel some of its movement. But the energy is blocked. This can lead us to feel stressed out, unfulfilled and unwell emotionally, relationally and physically.

EXERCISE: Feel the flow

Can you think of a time in your life where you were in flow and felt lifted beyond your usual parameters? Write about it. What can you learn from this transcendent moment?

Change the world

Rosa Parks couldn't understand why black people and white people were treated differently in her home state of Alabama. One day, Rosa refused to give up her seat to a white person just because she was black. With this small act, she rebelled against the racism hard-baked into the culture.[9] Rosa not only refused to submit to the story of white privilege – by staying in her seat, she created an as-yet-untold story.

This small act changed American society forever.

---

9   Biography, 'Rosa Parks' (A&E Television Networks, 2021),
     www.biography.com/activist/rosa-parks, accessed 12 May 2021

In big stories, there's the moment where the heroine crosses the threshold into a new world. They're not going to keep going round and round in the never-ending circles of a small story. They're not going to continue self-medicating and suppressing. They're going to turn and face their fears and sources of pain. They're motivated enough and their goal is big enough that they'll risk taking that first small step into the unknown in pursuit of a solution.

Final thoughts

It's easy for people to get stuck, maybe for the whole of their life, in small, bad stories that limit and constrict them. This book will show you how to break free of these stories and live the best story for you. A story of freedom from fear. A story that's an expression of your unique identity.

FIVE

Role

For any actor, taking on a role means stepping into another way of living. This often means facing parts of themselves that they'd rather avoid. But it doesn't stop there. An actor has a particularly mindful relationship with their inner wounds and painful memories. Rather than being controlled by these old stories and the painful events that triggered them, they use them as impetus to bounce into something new. They pivot into expressing some of those stories in the context of a role. This not only connects them with core narratives – it also allows them to use these narratives as energy for creating something new.

Let's look at how stepping into a role can be a helpful tool for sparking change in our lives.

Stepping into a role

Playing a role is ultimately a physical, not an intellectual, action. It means engaging with new possibilities in the body, in movement and through voice as much as thinking. Real change has to be physical as well as cognitive. A lot of our old stories lurk in our tired bodies, our collapsed posture and our tense muscles. As we step into a new story, a new way of being, we also take the journey through these physical habits and into a new form of embodiment. This means we connect to all aspects of ourselves, good and bad, and then move on from these places. In my experience, the physical shifts required for a new role won't last unless we also become more aware of the feelings and memories held in our bodies. This process is called stepping into a role.

Our new role isn't divorced from who we were up until now. Quite the reverse. Your new role is a fuller expression of who you already were all along. A few techniques can help you in this shift. They may seem superficial, but we know that even small changes on the outside can trigger big changes on the inside.

I know that when I wear a suit jacket, I feel more like a boss than I do in my joggers. Costume matters. Physicality matters.

Masks

I remember my first mask class as if it were yesterday. Each of us was given a different mask. Every mask had a different and exaggerated feature, one a long chin, another a beaked nose, another a look of wide-eyed innocence. Each mask was like a trigger for the expression of a different aspect of the actor wearing it. They magnified and emphasised different traits such as curiosity, lust, greed or innocence. I looked at my half mask, put it on and felt an immediate transformation. It felt as though the mask were magnifying one trait at a time, such as inquisitiveness and greediness, and each trait had a different way of moving attached to it. I was amazed at how easily and quickly the mask helped me slip into these traits.

Another exercise was based in the *commedia dell'arte* approach from medieval Italian theatre. Masks are often used in this theatrical tradition, but in my drama class, we emphasised just one aspect of the body and allowed that to lead us around the rehearsal room. It was interesting to realise that being led by the stomach would indeed foster a gluttonous and greedy character or being led by the forehead an endlessly curious and inquisitive character.

EXERCISE: Express yourself

See how quickly you can open up and express different aspects of yourself by trying one of these exercises.

- Walk around the room allowing yourself to be led by different parts of the body (forehead, nose, stomach or chin, for example). Observe how that feels.

- Write down different emotions, such as sadness, anger, surprise or fear, on pieces of paper (one on each piece of paper). Then choose a piece of paper at random and walk round your room as if you're the very manifestation of that feeling.

- Take note of what persona you're expressing when you dress in different styles of clothing.

These exercises are examples of the most primitive forms of entering into role.

The idea of role has been linked to masks or personas since the time of Greek theatre. A role is only visible via what a person does. The costume or colours we wear can act as a mask, which obscures some aspects of who we are while highlighting others. Even wearing a hat can make a difference to the way we feel about ourselves and how others react to us. The role can also change or open us up to aspects of ourselves that would otherwise remain dormant. We tend to express only a narrow range of roles in day-to-day identity. Acting releases us from these constrictions. Our identity tends to depend on emphasising some aspects of ourselves and burying their shadows, or opposites. Many stories are about the hero having to face parts of themselves they tried to bury or suppress. Role gives us a free pass to enter all these aspects of ourselves and connect with them. Roles we play can help us release and express different – sometimes surprisingly different – aspects of ourselves.

And roles help us navigate relationships with others. It's hard to even have a conversation unless you know the roles you and the other person are in.

In screenwriting, character traits are shown in the actions a character takes and their interactions with others. We may think about our character as something deeply embedded in the depths of our souls. From a spiritual perspective, I very much agree that we have a unique centre, a soul or heart – the core operating system for human beings. But this is really a theological and psychological perspective on character. In terms of dramatic storytelling, character is revealed only by what people do, particularly in relation to other people. At the heart of dramatic storytelling is action, and action tells us all we need to know about characters and, more importantly, who we are.

Subtext

Sometimes there's a discrepancy between what the character says and what they do, or between what they really feel and what they do. This is called subtext. This is the character as they really are underneath their actions. This adds complexity to the character and makes them compelling and interesting. It might seem to contradict what I'm saying about character being all about action, but it doesn't. From an acting perspective, you're still 'playing' the underlying subtext. It might not come up in words or external actions, but the audience will see it in small movements and 'tells', such as eye movement.

When I was at drama school, I had to play the role of the dauphin in *Henry V*. This was a high-status prince who spoke in the language of the court. But I decided to wear a donkey jacket and played him as low status. My director picked up that the subtext I was playing was producing a different character to the one in the play. They didn't appreciate my creativity!

Physicality is a key part of character. The social psychologist Amy Cuddy has done some interesting studies on the way that our posture reveals a lot about our character. When I was playing the dauphin as a stooped-over guy with a donkey jacket, I was playing out my own low-status narrative. Cuddy shows that as we expand and energise our physical posture, we also invite others to see us as a higher-status character.[10]

CASE STUDY – BILL

A client called Bill had a laid-back, nothing-matters, calm persona. He meditated, he looked after his health and he avoided alcohol. So why was he seeing me? He'd woken up one night convinced he was having a heart attack. Doctors checked him out and concluded that he

---

10 A Cuddy, *Presence: Bringing your boldest self to your biggest challenges* (Hachette, 2016)

was having panic attacks. This was a total mystery to Bill. He didn't do panic.

And yet, as he sat in front of me, his hands were constantly moving, he never looked settled and his thoughts about his life were full of fear and a dread that maybe he hated his job and struggled to see meaning in his life.

The subtext was screaming at me, and it contradicted the surface persona. Once he found creative and safe ways to express and face these feelings, his anxiety levels dropped significantly.

EXERCISE: Examine your subtext

Can you think of situations where you feel or think something that's different from what you express?

A subtext is often a suppressed need or want. What needs or wants are you most likely to hide from others?

What could happen if you expressed the subtext?

Status

One key way to identify what kind of role you habitually play is to think in terms of status. Everyone tends to gravitate toward a higher- or lower-status role in life. While status can be partly determined by our background, we can shift our status more than we realise. Someone playing a high-status role will be assertive but not aggressive about their needs and will value themselves in relationships with others.

Think about an interaction you had with someone today. What role were you portraying in terms of status? If a witness saw the interaction, how would they perceive your role?

Is this the kind of character you want to be? If not, what kind of character would you rather be?

Status is connected to energy and power. If you're low status, your energy will be low and your power reduced. Physically, this might look like hunched shoulders, a stooped posture and a general sense of the body collapsing toward the floor. Higher-status people aren't necessarily wealthy or of high social standing, but they do have influence and power. They have a higher level of energy that's inspiring to others and has an upward movement.

Which are you?

Goals

All characters or roles in stories have a desire – they want something, and their pursuit of that thing shapes their behaviour and choices. It's beyond what they currently have and motivates them into action. The goal could be to feed their family or earn a million. It creates energy and expectation. When an actor takes on a new role, they will often explore what the 'wants' are and what their goal is.

I like to describe goals using this imagery. An archer is just about to fire their arrow at a big round target. The direction the archer faces, the shape of their body and the action of releasing the arrow are all motivated by the target – not just an internal feeling but an external target.

Are you clear on what your target is in life?

Goals can be internal as well as external. An internal goal might involve realising the potential of the true self or healing an old wound. This deeper goal tends to be revealed as the story unfolds. At first, though, the goal is often to solve an external problem or win an external prize. As the story moves forward, the internal need for healing, integration and greater harmony comes through.

EXERCISE: Dive deep

Take some time to focus on one thing you want to see happen in your life. Get as specific as possible. Now consider these questions.

- How will this one thing change your relationships with others and yourself?
- What will a day in your life look like once you receive this one thing?

- What is your first step toward getting it?
- Who could your allies be in getting it?

What do you want and why?

Meaning

Any role has to have an objective, a focal point to aim for. Without this the role loses meaning and purpose. If, as an actor, I don't know the purpose that drives my role then I will struggle to know what gives each particular character a sense of meaning. The stories we live out are full of meaning. Some stories address questions regarding why we're here and the meaning of life. These may offer spiritual or theological explanations. Other stories will be inherited from our family and culture. These will highlight certain values and priorities that we should adhere to. Meaning is deeply woven into the fabric of our stories.

When we hit a turning point in life, or something disrupts our balance, the first instinct will be to use our old stories to make sense of what's happening and figure out what to do about it. This may help, but if the disruption is great enough, the old stories won't work. We won't be able to make sense of what's happening or know what to do about it.

We are meaning-making creatures. If our current story can't cope with reality, we'll become stressed out or develop a new story. It's at this point that people often seek therapy or coaching. Without a sense of meaning, we fall into chaos and depression.

Stories often work through the question of meaning. Sometimes the meaning the hero starts the story with is too superficial to survive the challenges that come. This can lead to a new understanding of what brings meaning.

Story doesn't simply tell us the meaning of life – it gives us building blocks that we can engage with emotionally, as if the narrative is really happening, so we can make our own meaning out of the experience.

In good stories, different people will have different ideas around meaning and also come to different real-isations about meaning at different times. Parables in the Bible are good examples of mini-stories that can bear different meanings at different times. They act as symbols onto which we project meaning and order.

It's easy to find ourselves in relationships, jobs, roles and situations which don't give us a sufficient sense of meaning and purpose. Again, if this is you, it may be time to switch up the story.

When I was first looking for work, I interviewed for a job with an insurance company. When asked why I was there, I said, 'Because my dad made me come.' I could think of nothing worse than being an actuary. I wanted to be in a rock band. Insurance had no meaning for me. If I'd gotten this job, I would have struggled against the tide of a job that was meaningless to me.

Final thoughts

This act has been a bit like opening up a clock and seeing how all the working mechanisms fit together to produce a timepiece. In this case we have looked at the components of story; how some stories are better than others, and the outworking of these stories in the roles we play. To take the analogy further, you could say that the story is the clock's working mechanism, and the role is the hands on the clock. In life, it is often the role someone is playing that we notice first, but there is always a story behind the role, shaping and directing it, for better or worse. Now we have a better understanding of story and role we can move to Act Two where we start to create, rehearse and play out new stories and roles for our lives.

ACT TWO
REHEARSING
NEW STORIES

SIX

Preparing To Live A New Story

Welcome to the rehearsal room!

As an actor, I learned that taking on a new character, telling a new story and relating to others in that story was a process that took time, energy and work. The same is required to change our life story and the roles we play. Act Two focuses on the somewhat mysterious and alchemic world of the rehearsal process. This is where the methods of transformation come to the fore. This is the crucible of change, the pivot point.

The first part of this process is letting go of our habitual ways of thinking, moving and relating. This is necessary if we are to step into new patterns. But I want to reassure you – this book isn't about making you an actor. It's also not just about pretending or 'faking it till you make it'. Maybe there is an element of pretend, but whenever we put on any type of costume or move in a different way, we'll quickly find that some new character will just pop up. It's as if there are other stories and characters within us, just waiting for the invitation to appear. Children do this instinctively, but under the right conditions, adults can also shapeshift in a second. When this happens, we aren't being fake. We're tapping into something real and true. There are many authentic parts of ourselves we aren't aware of and never utilise. The tools in this section will help you do that.

You are not the old story

This is *very* important. As discussed, we develop self-narratives and their associated roles in response to life events. These narratives feel like unquestionable truth, yet they're shaped by unique events and how we narrate these events to ourselves. I have twin daughters. They're as close as it's possible to be genetically, and they had the same upbringing. But they've developed their own unique and specific narratives and identities. During the Blitz in WWII, some people were traumatised and some rose to the challenge and carried on cheerfully. 'True life' stories are much less connected to only one way of interpreting life than they seem to be. This means that we can always shift to a new narrative that would cause us to interpret the events of our lives quite differently. Whatever story you've been telling about yourself isn't the final word on who you are. Shifting out of old stories is simply a matter of perspective.

Let's return to the example of the book *Room*. The four-year-old protagonist was born in the room and knows nothing of the outside world. But there's a whole world outside this narrative that is real yet invisible to him. This plot serves as a good analogy. We can all get stuck in our own rooms. It's easy to think our experience defines our story. Who we really are, the story and role we're discovering, is so much deeper and stronger than anything we've been through.

What parts of the old story do you want to keep?

That said, there may be parts of the old story that are important to hold on to. We don't have to abandon all aspects of our old stories, even if they were quite toxic and negative. There may have also been some helpful aspects to them.

Even though an 'all is lost moment' is commonly part of the story of transformation, some aspects of the previous life can still be threaded into future narratives. When I work with people who are dealing with a catastrophic loss, I try to find some threads of the past that they can pull through into the future tapestry they're weaving.

It's worth considering what you value in the life you've lived to this point. Which relationships, activities, ways of being and even objects do you want to take with you into the future? Remember: transformation is usually an evolution rather than a revolution.

Sources for new stories

Where are the new stories going to come from? Actors use their imagination to access stories. They reconfigure bits and pieces of their own lives and cannibalise them to fit the new story, the new role. I'm not suggesting that, as authors of our own lives, we do this in an individualistic way. We are creatures of co-construction who build our stories in partnership and dialogue with others. To inspire this process, ask friends, 'What are the top three most inspiring things you see in my life?' This is a legitimate basis on which to start weaving a new story. In my experience, people in our networks, including friends and even work colleagues, can be helpful when it comes to discovering stories that pull us past our self-enforced limitations.

Now let's push the envelope. What if the writer of our story was God (or whatever you call your higher power)? What would it be like to listen to this story and find out what it is? Is there a better, truer story that God wants to use your life to tell?

New stories can be woven from the cloud of story and narrative by which we're always surrounded (books, TV, film and the stories of our culture). They can also come from the worst moments in our old story. Sometimes these are called redemptive narratives. These moments can be transformed into pivot points that unlock new stories, which lead to new ways of being. Unless we use old negative stories as a spring-board into something alive and passionate, they'll keep pulling us back down – back into being stuck. If we can incorporate the shadow parts of our life and create gold out of the darkness, we can write deep and sustainable stories that remain resilient in the face of setbacks.

I once had a strong story about being an unwanted outsider. When I repurposed this story into one of being a visionary with an ability to see life from a unique perspective, I shifted the narrative. The core narrative remained – that I operate on the margins of the mainstream – but now it's a tool for good, not bad.

The cost of change

Having looked at your old story, you might conclude that it needs an upgrade. It might not be fit for pur-pose in the life you live now. It might even be toxic and unhelpful. Maybe it's based on avoiding further disappointment or pain rather than embracing all that life has for you.

For real change to happen, there needs to be a compelling reason. The cost of staying the same must be greater than the cost of changing. Sometimes this looks like 'hitting rock bottom'. You don't have to hit rock bottom, but unless you have a reason to change, you'll probably continue in familiar patterns and habits.

EXERCISE: Consider the costs

Find a piece of paper and draw a line down the middle. On one side, write the cost of staying as you are. On the other, write the cost of changing. This will likely be fairly unknown right now, but it's still worth considering at this stage. It will give you an accurate picture of how prepared and motivated you actually are to make the necessary changes.

Head to heart

As a psychotherapist, I often find the limitations of a speech-based medium frustrating. Talking about things is certainly helpful. Words can and do change cultures. They can bring war or peace. But many of the traumas that people carry around in their hearts sit below the level of language. Cognitive-based conversation (most therapy) might not reach far enough below the surface to engage with old and toxic stories held in the body and unconscious mind.

Our earliest ways of making sense of the world come not via language but movement and physical interaction with others. Our stories are shaped by the quality of how our parents look at us and by the way we are held (or not). Our identity and sense of self begins with the quality of the physical relationship with a parent, not with concepts and words. I wasn't held, looked at or touched by a parent for the first two weeks of life, and this undoubtedly left me with a fragile sense of self and zero sense of worth. No surprise that I grew up anxious and insecure. This then became the basis for the story I told myself about the world (unsafe), others (abandoning) and myself (unlovable).

So it seems logical to me that if we want to change our identity roles and the stories we tell, we have to reach back into our hearts, our felt experience, and incorporate the physical. When I'm acting, I might know the story of my character, but it's all hypothetical until I physically inhabit that role. To develop new stories and roles, we need to tap into our hearts and bodies. By heart, I refer to that part of us that generates emotions – and these are experienced physically. It's also the heart that makes snap assessments about the world. We're often only dimly aware of our hearts, and yet if we don't engage them in this process, we'll be unlikely to change anything.

Part of the rehearsal process is accessing and drawing on our hearts and getting out of our heads. We'll now look at some ways we can start to get out of our own way.

Mindfulness

In my work as a coach, therapist and spiritual director, I often see people taking the 'try harder' approach to changing themselves. You may have tried this yourself. This is when you decide you'd like to be a different kind of person and that you'll adopt new character traits, new thinking, new behaviours and so on. Many people will identify old thought patterns and contradict them with more 'rational' thoughts. This can be helpful, but in my experience, old scripts and narratives are hard to weed out. You pull a narrative up here and another one breaks through over there.

I recommend a different approach. Rather than rushing into making new stories, we need to gently release ourselves from old ones. This isn't meant to be a fight against ourselves. It's more like being aware of the old narrative – seeing it and then not reacting to it. Essentially, this is mindfulness. There are many great resources on mindfulness if you wish to study the approach, but in a nutshell, it's the practice of noticing our thoughts without reacting to them. I use an embodied version of mindfulness with my clients. This means not only being aware of thoughts but also feelings, both emotional and physical. If you're not sure what you're feeling emotionally, pay attention to physical sensations – for example, areas of tension or even pain in the body are often linked to emotional states. The key idea is to not fight, replace or challenge these thoughts and feelings but gently notice them and choose to let them pass through. Here's an image that might help: imagine standing on a riverbank and letting little boats of thoughts and feelings float downstream without jumping onto one of the boats.

This kind of mindfulness is essential when detoxing from our old stories and roles. It's also a great way to create more mind space for new stories and roles. If we don't clear the clutter, it's going to be difficult to have enough rehearsal space to practice the new stories and roles.

I recommend practicing this mindfulness approach for twenty minutes each day. It will put you in a better position to take on new stories.

Soul music

Our souls are the operating systems that hold everything together – our minds, bodies, spirits, and hearts. Our souls always know what's true and will never lie to us. They're the grid that links and interconnects everything about who we are. I believe the soul is tuned into the spiritual world that some describe as the universe, a higher power or God. The soul is where the language of story makes the most sense and also from where it originates. This is because the soul can relate to our hearts and minds, to our bodies and spirits.

I'm not in the business of replacing one dysfunctional narrative for something slightly less toxic. I'm interested in going deeper and connecting with the soul as the source of all narrative, imagination and role. This is the true foundation from which we're free to make any number of authentic and life-affirming stories.

With mindfulness, we free ourselves of the white noise of thoughts and fears. But what is it that we're making contact with once things go quiet? Some would say that we're no more than the narratives we tell, that there is no fundamental self or soul, unique to the individual. I disagree. I think we do have an operating system, or soul, which knows the truth about us and is inherently connected to the universe, spirit and others. The soul has massive potential and is capable of more than we can imagine. It is physical and spiritual and certainly not a disembodied or split-off part of us.

So what are we getting in touch with when we get in touch with the soul?

For most of my life, I was driven by my ego. This is that part of us that lives in fear of 'getting it wrong' and goes into overdrive to please others or avoid the shame of failure. The ego is the source of what I described earlier as bad stories. My ego was based on the story that I wasn't enough and would only be acceptable if I helped others. I figured out how people ticked, how I ticked. I did a lot of therapy, worked in psychiatry and became a psychotherapist. I sought out applause and glamour by going to drama school and becoming an actor. I became a spiritual teacher and got ordained as a priest. But I was still displaced from my soul and in a state of perpetual deficit. It was only when I was finally able to break through the clouds of my addictions and false narratives that I saw something else. Something that had been with me all along: my soul.

And here's the thing. I realised my soul was doing fine. It wasn't damaged like my heart, full of pain and false stories. And here's *the* thing. My soul, just like yours, is rooted in love. When we wake up to this truth, we find what has been there all along. Love. The universe is running on a spirit of love, and love means we're never alone. Our souls are always in a dance that embraces others at the deepest level. We need to take time to connect with our souls, to breathe in the love that's available as we step away from old narratives.

If you're anything like me, this idea that love is at the root of everything may seem rather inaccessible. I spent most of my life working on the assumption that the only love I'd get would be earned. I found the concept of being loved unconditionally as foreign as a trip to Mars. But there were a few things that helped me to access this truth. The first was the fact that, like any new script, the script of love has to be practiced and embodied.

EXERCISES: Get in touch with your soul

1. Imagine that you're utterly loved and held by a 'higher power'. Feel what this does to your body.

2. Imagine that the air around you is love – love directed at you and demanding nothing. How do you move through such an atmosphere?

3. Find pieces of music or film clips that put you in mind of love and spend time with these on a daily basis. Make a mix tape based on love that really works for you.

4. Start performing random acts of kindness for others. This will put you in touch with your soul.

The soul can reshape the mind and change our deepest assumptions. Connecting with the soul enables us to develop authentic new narratives and roles. The soul is the platform from which they flow. When I started to acclimatise to being in touch with my soul and love, the need to be accepted or loved by others stopped driving my narratives and roles. Being in touch with soul doesn't stop us from generating narratives and roles. It does mean we can more easily access power, energy, creativity and authenticity. If we live from our souls, rather than our fearful and anxious and grasping egos, we can take a more dialogic approach to life and avoid getting trapped by any one story. When we get in touch with the soul, we get in touch with love.

Final thoughts

In this chapter we have prepared the ground for new stories and roles to be built upon. So often I have seen people fail to transform their lives from lack of preparation. So, we have counted the cost of changing and not changing as well as deciding what parts of the old story to keep. This chapter has also focused on the importance of new stories that connect with and express our hearts and souls. Mindful practice helps clear the space for these connections to happen.

SEVEN

Rediscovering The Lost Art Of Play

To create a new story and role, we must be able to play. Let's dive into this idea.

Play

When I was young, I played games in the school playground based on whatever my favourite TV show at the time was. My friends and I would make up stories and fight over who was going to be the 'goodie' and the 'baddie' that day. At no point did we sit down and have a meeting about how we were going to construct a three-act narrative and believable characters. We just jumped in and did it. We worked out the story as we enacted our roles.

As I grew up, my play became much more considered and premeditated. I remember planning an attack on a climbing frame. I was ten. I had a diagram of where everyone in my schoolyard gang was going to go in this planned assault. I accept now that this may have been a little over-controlling.

As we get older, our play becomes more formalised and cognitive. We work out plans in our minds before executing them. This is quite normal. But if we build up narratives and roles in reaction to life that are rigid and defensive, we may find ourselves a long way from the playground and instead oscillating between two polarities. I've found this to be particularly true of people with addictive tendencies. At one extreme there's an overreliance on ego-driven thinking. This is a drive to get things right and control anything that gets in the way. It's intolerant and narcissistic. But the stress of trying to live from the head, without the heart, can also trigger a fall into mindless activities, such as gaming or watching porn or drinking alcohol. This is the other extreme. These things create an external structure, and they can make us feel euphoric.

But this isn't play. It may feel like it, but it isn't. It may engage fantasy while bypassing healthy imagination.

Rediscovering play is essential if we are to try on new narratives and roles. Play happens when mind, heart and body are integrated and acting together. It's soul work. Thought, emotion and physicality are all involved. To play, we have to get unstuck from fear, old stories and dead rules.

Rediscovering our innate ability to play is not childish. It's essential for individuals, for businesses and for wider society. So often play is subcontracted to online-content platforms. We become an audience to a show performed by others. Inability to play closes people down, reduces creativity and can lead to a general feeling of being stuck. Play depends on flexibility of storytelling and role playing. Once life has got someone stuck in a defensive story, role play becomes impossible. Learning to play again unlocks us from parts of us that have got stuck or frozen. It reminds us who we are.

Safe vulnerability

For many years, I had a fear of going on the subway (or, as we call it in London, the Underground) because I once got stuck in an overcrowded railway carriage on the way to drama school. I was trapped in the sticky silence for forty-five minutes, and that trauma stayed with me. After this, whenever a train slowed down or stopped between stations, my heart rate went up and I felt all the symptoms of rising panic, including dry mouth, clammy hands and shallow breathing. I couldn't read, couldn't think and most definitely couldn't be creative. Under the flattening weight of stress, all my usual forms of play, such as writing in my journal, thinking about ideas for a book or running through storylines for a potential film, were impossible.

To be free to play and be vulnerable, you need boundaries.

Play won't happen without safety – and knowing the boundaries or rules of the game provides this. The game could be in the playground or the corporate boardroom. Not knowing the rules of the system we're in is inherently stressful, and it hinders creative thinking and play. So it's important that these boundaries are created if they're not already there. This might mean getting up an hour earlier to write in your journal or get to the gym. It might mean saying no to activities that, while good, might distract from time set aside to play.

Play might take the form of watching a show or playing a sport or shopping with friends. These are all great. But it would be helpful to extend yourself, at least for a while, more intentionally into creative activities such as art, drama or music. I can't tell you the number of young adults I see who feel a deep sadness as a result of neglecting their creative passions. I recently spoke to an artist who was working in the corporate world and hadn't picked up a paintbrush for years. He felt something was missing. And he was right.

If we are to change our story and live out a new identity, we have to learn to play again. This isn't something just for 'creative' types – play is a core element of human nature. But first, we need to establish boundaries. One of the core aspects of rehearsal for actors is building up trust with other actors and feeling confident to try out new ideas. It is important for all of us to find relationships, groups and networks in which we can try on different costumes and stories and laugh at ourselves when we get it wrong. This could be a solo pursuit, but it's ideal to play with others.

Vulnerability keeps us in touch with our hearts and souls and open to the experience of others. That said, there are blocks to vulnerability. Brené Brown has talked about how shame in particular blocks us from being vulnerable.[11] We fear looking silly, being criticised, making a mistake. All these things will kill play. Part of vulnerability is a willingness to let other people participate. If we react to others with control and fear, we're unable to play.

CASE STUDY – GEORGE

George, a church leader, was an amazing teacher and more spiritual than anyone else, at least as far as his congregation was concerned. Of course this was all a persona, a mask. Behind this was a terrified child hoping no one would discover the hideous truth: that he had no clue what he was doing, didn't really believe in God and was addicted to porn.

---

11   B Brown, *Rising Strong* (Penguin, 2015)

As we spoke, George started to creep out from behind his persona. He shared his truth with me and discovered that being vulnerable didn't trigger a bolt of lightning or, even worse, make me criticise or shame him. The fear of being shamed and humiliated can be worse than the fear of death. This is why some people say they're more afraid of public speaking than death. It's the shame that kills.

The day George finally started to live as his authentic self, rather than a cardboard cut-out of others' expectations, was the day he stood up in front of his church and shared his doubts and struggles. Vulnerability starts with being able to let ourselves 'fail' according to the laws we've placed over our lives. Vulnerability and safety are two sides of the same coin.

EXERCISE: Two sides of the same coin

Think of one area of your life where you could increase your safety, perhaps utilising boundaries.

Think of one relationship where you could increase your vulnerability.

Kiss the demon on the lips

I have a friend who uses this phrase. It means facing our shadow and connecting with it rather than running from it or projecting it onto others and running from them.

Play allows us to step out of our public persona, which often involves people-pleasing and being good, nice or non-offensive. Play allows us to engage with the darker and more 'unacceptable' parts of ourselves. In the journey to play new roles and tell new stories, we may have to confront aspects of ourselves that we'd rather leave buried.

Many of my clients with eating disorders desperately wanted to be 'good'. This was an ego-driven and ultimately hopeless desire to rise above the parts of themselves they couldn't tolerate. Although my clients thought this drive for the perfect body or perfect life was admirable, it was in fact killing them. In a society that's saturated in images of thin women who 'have it all', a lethal link has been made between success and being a size zero. And so, many intelligent young women (and men) play out a catastrophic narrative: that their worth and value is utterly dependent on their looking a certain way.

Family, friends and even clinicians often understand this as an issue of control. Actually, it's an issue of abject fear. What are they afraid of? The same thing that most of us are afraid of. Themselves. Or at least certain aspects of themselves. The parts kept in the shadow. Unfortunately, the more we suppress these messy, chaotic and undesirable parts of ourselves, the more we suppress the energy and reality of who we are.

When working in a regional adolescent unit near Liverpool early in my career, I found that drama is excellent at helping people get in touch with these unacceptable parts of themselves. The most inhibited and withdrawn kid could flourish into a boss gangster while in a role. Why? Because of the power of the 'as if' reality. Drama provides many vehicles for giving voice to these 'bad' bits of the self. These vehicles include puppets, masks, costume, bits of text from plays or films and even make-up. It's incredible how liberating even small shifts in our everyday role are. Have you ever tried putting on new make-up or a hat that's just a little different from your norm? On a small scale, this is like shifting into another role or story. It also releases a part of you that was perhaps hiding.

My clients with anorexia had to get into a dialogue with those parts of themselves that they hated and feared. They did this partly by putting language to their feelings but also by doing creative exercises such as drawing an outline of their bodies and then filling it in with words and colours – the emotional content stuck in their physicality. Drama, imagination and shifts in role are effective at opening up dialogue between the ego-driven person and their own hearts. Sometimes this literally saves lives.

EXERCISES: Found objects and empty chairs

Go for a walk and find something that captures your attention. It may be a flower, a rock, a piece of garbage.

Whatever it is, try to notice the object's details. What is its weight? How does it feel? Colour? Shape? Does it evoke any feelings (on the whole, though, keep your observations practical). Write all this down.

Then read over what you've written. Every time you wrote either the name of the object or 'it', replace that with 'I'. Sometimes there can be an uncanny link between the details of your found object and aspects of yourself.

Now try the empty-chair exercise, which therapists often use. Imagine a key person in your life is sitting in a chair opposite you. Ask their advice about something. Then move to that chair and start speaking as if you were them. This can quickly open us up to parts of ourselves that may have great wisdom to impart.

Same event, different story

One way we can start to shift and change our stories is to take an event and notice the story we're telling about it. For example, you may be in heavy traffic. You could see it as a colossal waste of time and get frustrated. Or you could see it as an opportunity to make some calls and catch up with people you haven't spoken to for ages. Same situation, different story.

EXERCISE: Finding the positives

Whatever situation you're in now as you read this, wherever you are, whoever you're with and whatever else is happening in your day, take thirty seconds and do this:

Think of the worst story you could tell about what's happening to you now.

Then, without changing the facts of your situation, think of the best story you could tell about this moment (maybe as you look back on it five years from now).

Making friends with disruption

The COVID-19 pandemic brought about much disorder and disruption. If there's too much disruption, we can become traumatised and even frozen with anxiety. But a certain amount of stress is helpful to move us into change.

CASE STUDY – SIMON

Simon was addicted to porn for twenty years. It was his go-to form of self-soothing. Whenever he felt stressed, anxious, sad or angry, he'd dive into the internet. He got to a point in his recovery where he was able to stop replaying the script in which porn was the answer to any and every problem.

Then something strange and new started to happen. Simon felt disorientated and 'not himself'. This was because, in a sense, he was no longer his 'old self'. His old self was held together by his addiction, and as his addiction started to fade, he went through a period of disorientation, of readjustment.

This is usually a brief and temporary state and is common when people make deep shifts out of their old state of mind and narrative.

In this creative rehearsal process, there must be some embracing of disorder and disruption. Otherwise, we can get stuck in our old ways of doing things. Disruption of the old narrative precedes the establishing of a new story. In acting rehearsals, directors will sometimes use games and exercises to disrupt the actor and free them to take on a new role. There are many ways you could disrupt your old habits.

- Take a different route home from work or a friend's place.

- Play music that's different from what you usually listen to.

- Say hello to someone you wouldn't usually speak to.

- Wear different clothes.

Pick one!

Get clear on what you really want

Actors are often preoccupied with understanding what their character wants in a scene. It's these objectives that motivate and energise their behaviour. When it comes to any kind of life transformation or personal growth, we need a target, an objective. Remember the archer imagery from Chapter 5? The bullseye we focus on will shape us in a particular way. In the context of this book, that shape is a new narrative and role. We'll explore how to develop a new narrative and role, but first we need an external and future-orientated objective. It's hard to construct a role or story if we don't know what the point of it all is.

So what's the bullseye you're aiming for?

I've lost count of the number of clients who've have described their objectives to me in these terms:

- 'I just want things to go back to the way they were.'

- 'I want the pain and suffering to stop.'

- 'I don't want any more fear and stress.'

- 'I don't want this kind of relationship any more.'

The problem with these statements is that they're not objectives. An objective isn't the absence of something. It's a positive and concrete thing that's yet to be achieved but is also measurable and easy to define.

It's possible you may have different objectives in different aspects of your life – family, work, relationships, etc. For now, I'd like you to consider what objective you'd like to achieve in just one area of life.

Once positive objectives are established, it's easier to develop roles and narratives that aim toward achieving them. For example, writing this book has meant getting up early in the morning to do my pages. But it also means assuming the identity of a writer.

Having an objective also helps you sort out what's important to you and clarifies your primary focus. I can easily get distracted by a variety of projects. Having a clear and single objective helps me to keep the main thing the main thing. This saves a lot of time and wasted energy. Having an objective is a kind of boundary that limits and focuses the range of our new narrative and role.

So what's the one thing you want to make your number-one priority in the next day, week or month?

Final thoughts

In this chapter we have unpacked some different aspects of play. New stories and roles will flourish best in an atmosphere of playfulness. To enable this to happen means creating safe places in which to be vulnerable, being clear on what we want and making friends with disruption.

EIGHT

Build A New Story

W e now come to the question at the heart of this book. How can you write a new life story? We'll look at some keys to building a new story and pivoting into a new life.

Bounce off the narrative

I don't believe we can simply superimpose a new story on top of deep-rooted origin stories that define the way we see ourselves, others and our world. Often these narratives are formed in response to pain and self-defensiveness. If we are to transform our story, we'll need to come face to face with these often-negative stories and the pain that caused them. This can be uncomfortable. In story language, I link this with the 'all is lost' moment. This is the part of the narrative which feels like defeat and yet is also the point where everything can change. It may feel overwhelmingly negative, but it's out of this 'dark night of the soul' that new light starts to emerge. This is where the bounce-back begins, which in turn triggers breakthrough and victory. Once we've identified our toxic, bad stories, we can bounce off them into something new.

The simplest way to do this is to start creating a new story that is the exact opposite of the old one. When I work through this with clients, it never ceases to amaze me how quickly they can find themselves seeing things completely differently. What's more, the new story feels more authentic in terms of who they are.

We begin by calling out the 'problem tales' that many of us drag around like a thick cloud of negativity. These can be cripplingly limiting to individuals, organisations, businesses and churches. They contain these kinds of statements:

- 'We've tried everything and nothing works.'

- 'Everyone said I'd never amount to anything.'

- 'It's always been this way and nothing I do can change it.'

- 'No one ever listens to me.'

- 'I don't deserve to be loved.'

- 'I'll never be good in business.'

And so on. As you read these, you may feel a slight sinking feeling. These narratives can easily become a dark vortex pulling all light and life into them.

EXERCISE: Start a new story

Identify some of your core narratives by completing these sentences:

I am...

The world is...

People are...

I always...

...will never happen for me.

Then write the opposite of all your statements. This could be the start of bouncing into a new story.

How do you feel about the opposite, more positive narratives?

Here's another exercise that can help you bounce back from old stories to new ones.

EXERCISE: Timelines

Draw a line. This is your life to date. Then mark on it the first three occasions that come to mind that were challenging or painful. Then write one line describing what story you might have told about yourself, others or the world as a consequence of the event. Take a moment to consider if this statement has influenced the rest of your life and the roles you play.

Then take each statement and work with it.

1. Think of a statement that is opposite to your bad story. Meditate on how you would play out this new statement. For example, in my case, I recently had to think about being at the centre of a team rather than being Mr Invisible complaining on the sidelines. I had to contradict the thought that kept popping into my mind that I was invisible and irrelevant. So I visualised being influential and decisive.

2. Ask God or the universe to give you another perspective on your old story. Remember that however we understand the spiritual dimension, above all, it's about love, acceptance and peace. What does your higher power say about you and your responses to each painful event? Is there another way of telling this story? This isn't about denying the pain or injustice of difficult life experiences – it's an opportunity to hear another perspective. When I did this exercise, I had a strong sense that God celebrated my birth and lifted me up for the world to see.

Build new statements about you, others and the world for each event.

If we listen to our intuition or God or the universe, we're going to pick up on a more benign and loving story than the ones rooted in our history. Alternative narratives have always been available to us, yet we could go a lifetime without accessing them, staying stuck in catastrophic narratives shaped by pain. Again, it's important to retell these core narratives, otherwise it's nigh on impossible to change the way we live and the roles we play out.

When you build new stories, don't forget to incorporate the best of the old ones. As mentioned, there will also be some good, helpful aspects of your old stories that you'll want to identify and keep. Some of the building blocks of your new story are probably sitting in your old one. When people are in a crisis or wanting to make big changes fast, I always suggest slowing the process down and seeing the assets and strengths that are already in play. Starting from scratch with an empty page doesn't work. The old stories will catch up with you. This is why New Year's resolutions are rarely effective.

Moving through the acts

An important part of being able to rewrite our life script is knowing where we are in the big story of our lives. Unless we know where we currently are, we cannot transition to the next stage.

Act 1

A lot of people come to see me for coaching when they hit what screenwriters would call the inciting incident.

This is when something happens and the wheels come off. It might be having an affair, being caught shoplifting or losing a job. As we saw in Chapter 1, this is Act 1. And this is where all my new clients are.

To move through Act 1, you'll need to do the following:

1. Find a way to manage the disruption.

2. Realise that the old ways of coping, all your old narratives, are useless now.

3. Stop numbing, self-medicating or distracting yourself from how you feel (through food, porn, alcohol, drugs, TV, gaming etc).

4. Accept that new solutions must be found.

5. Decide that avoiding change is now more damaging to you than taking a new path.

6. Step over the threshold and onto a new pathway. You'll need guides and allies for the journey into the unknown (therapists, mentors, friends, coaches, recovery programmes). And these people will need to know the path better than you.

Act 2

Act 2 is where we're engaged with trying something new and the messy and disorientating process of transformation. At this stage, new ideas will be tried and abandoned – keep going. I'd describe it as a rehearsal period, with all the chaos and embarrassing trial and error this represents. Failure is part of the process here. This is like the chrysalis stage of a caterpillar metamorphosing into a butterfly. Or you could think of it as being like going to the gym and breaking down muscle to build new muscle.

To move through Act 2, you'll need to do the following:

1. Allow your old assumptions and stories to be questioned and maybe unravel.

2. Accept the support and guidance of friends and mentors.

3. Allow yourself to get used to being vulnerable.

4. Move from chaos and distraction into one clear goal.

5. Surrender to a higher power. This means stepping back from the self you've built and into a space that could be described as transcendent or spiritual.

6. Realise that an 'all is lost' moment, when things seem to have slipped back to square one, is part of the process. It's darkest before the dawn!

7. Be ready to implement that killer idea that drops into your mind.

Act 3

Breaking into Act 3 means coming to a point where the world as you know it is surrendered. It's the point of letting go of old, ego-based ways of trying to control life and allowing something bigger to flow through you. If your life so far has been like a river, contained within the limits of riverbanks, in Act 3 the river moves into the sea – the sea of other people, the culture and the wider world. It's the part of the story where the hero, operating in the freedom and truth of their potential, starts to make the world a better place. Their hard-won insights and wisdom can now be used in the service of their networks, family and society. Act 3 starts with a big win. The obstacle that has stood in the way of meeting objectives has been overcome, the villain defeated and the hero's shadow confronted and integrated. There's then a return home followed by reintegration with society. Often the society must readjust to accommodate the changes in the hero.

To move through Act 3, you'll need to do the following:

1. Take action. Strike the killer blow. Win the prize. Achieve the goal. Overcome your nemesis.

2. Make the transition back into 'normal' life.

3. Look for ways to serve your culture with the wisdom and experience you now have.

4. Put habits in place that will sustain your new story and role.

Visualise your new story

Now we come to the final stage of making a new story.

EXERCISE: Building blocks

Make note of all the things from your past that you think are life-giving and that you want to keep in the new story.

Think of an objective that you'd like to achieve. It can be as far out as you want.

Now think of an internal obstacle you'll need to overcome to reach the objective. For example, I needed to stop ignoring my feelings and thinking of myself as having no worth.

Now imagine you woke up tomorrow and these changes had magically happened. What would your day look like? Visualise the usual challenges but see yourself dealing with them differently. It might help to recall moments in your past which resonate with what you're visualising.

These are the basic building blocks of living a new story that is bigger, richer, freer. One that more authentically expresses who you are.

I heard something interesting in a spin class one day. The instructor engaged the imagination and linked it to physical training. Usually these classes (which I'm terrified to attend) seem to consist of going up and down through the gears and rising up in the saddle. But this instructor said, 'Think of what gives you the most life, joy and hope. It might be the deal you're going to make this week, the date you can't wait for or your love for a partner or family member. Now let that energy power your movement.'

I loved this!

The instructor made a direct link between visualisation, positive energy and physical action. This is the living demonstration of a key principle. Imagination and visualisation enable us to access energy and momentum for forward movement and change. If we can't see it, we can't be it. Just as a target shapes our movement and stance, what we see in our imagination has a powerful effect on feelings and physicality.

Before we move on, I want to make a distinction between visualisation and fantasy.

Fantasy

Over the years, I've worked with many people who are addicted to porn. To a lesser extent, I've also met with people addicted to gaming. While these things certainly engage the imagination, I've come to believe that fantasy can be toxic and damaging. Why? Because fantasy usually avoids reality and tends to overwhelm us with powerful imagery which we don't construct but simply consume. Passive consumption can act as a tsunami of stimulating imagery that flattens and blunts our natural ability to use visualisation and imagination to create and shape new stories. Under these conditions, our minds can become passive and easily influenced. So much of my work is about helping clients move from fantasy into a healthy imagination that uses visualisation to create new stories to live out.

Visualisation

This is the conscious activation of the imagination in relation to forthcoming action. It's similar to the idea of setting an intention. It's 'seeing' concrete activity that can be felt in the body. For example, a runner might visualise a running track as part of their preparation to run the 100-metre dash. This process fires neurons in the brain as if the person were actually running the race. The brain can experience what is visualised as if it were really happening – imagination alone can release chemicals into the body and brain equivalent to those that would be produced if the visualisation were real. This underlines the power of this seeing part of our mind, which is essential when building new roles and stories.

You don't have to be 'creative' to visualise. This ability is hardwired into us. Often, we use visualisation to frighten ourselves with bad stories that may or may not happen. Instead, we could use this intrinsic skill to build good stories and a better future.

When an actor learns a new role, they need to visualise that character in all the scenes they inhabit. The mind and body will usually follow where the imagination leads. So how can we deploy our imagination to create life stories and the energy to enact these stories in new roles?

Here are some exercises that will serve as warm-ups to get you in the right zone for making changes to your story and the roles you play.

Visualisation exercises

Exercise 1

Visualise a part of your day that you're not looking forward to. Start by visualising your worst fear regarding how it could go. This may mean facing feelings you usually try to avoid, but remember that it's just a short exercise. As you go through the sequence of events, notice how you're feeling in different parts of your body. No need to change anything. Just notice.

In my experience with clients, I've found that just doing this exercise is enough to defuse the fear of that dreaded conversation or meeting. Their level of anxiety might shoot up initially, but it's not possible to remain at this peak level for too long. People realise that their fears are disproportionate to the situation itself. How many of us can agree that our worst fears almost never happen?

This exercise goes further than defusing the fear, though. Now visualise the same future situation going as well as it possibly could. Remember, this is about imagination and play, so don't worry if what you're visualising might be unrealistically positive. Notice how you feel physically as you visualise that part of your day going well. Again, this is the same process runners use when preparing for a big race. They visualise every corner, every part of the track, and as they do, their neurological pathways line up with their minds.

Exercise 2

Set aside five minutes at the start of your day to visualise every part of the day ahead. As you scan your diary, imagine that the day is going to go so much better than you could have dreamed. Notice how this makes you feel physically.

Then at the end of the day, scan over the day's events and pick out what can be celebrated. By doing this, you start to shift your narrative about life's daily events that so often feel as if they're happening 'to us'. This exercise will help you take a more empowered position in which you're writing your own narrative.

Exercise 3

You don't have to be religious or spiritual to do this. Take some time at the end of the day to ask yourself where a higher power was at work. This may look like coincidences, unexpected pleasures, chance meetings or moments of fun, satisfaction or even joy. Even if your day felt dark and grey and everything was a struggle, use your visualisation to see if there was something of God sitting alongside you in the shadows.

Exercises to wake up the imagination

Exercise 1

You can do this in a group or alone. Take any object (maybe a comb or a bottle) and imagine it becoming eight different objects. Then mime the use of each of these objects. For example, if you have a bottle and imagine it becoming a comb, you may push your hair back with the bottle. This can become a guessing game, like charades, if you do it with a partner or in a group.

Exercise 2

This is a bit more therapeutic, and it's great for telling a current or familiar story and then retelling and reshaping it super fast. This is a snapshot comparison between now and the desired future.

Take some small objects, such as buttons, stones from the garden or, if you're feeling particularly metaphorical, those farmyard animals you can get in a pick-and-mix box from the second-hand shop.

Then choose different objects to represent you and others in one of your current contexts (eg at work). Place the 'characters' on the table in such a way as to represent the relationships. So those characters who are emotionally more connected to each other would be positioned closer, and those who are far apart for one reason or another would be placed far apart from each other spatially. This quickly offers a helicopter perspective of the systemic narrative of that aspect of your life.

Next, shift the objects to show a map of the story you'd like to tell. Would you like to be closer to some people? Further away?

Now consider this: what is the first thing you can do to move the picture from the first to the second configuration?

Exercise 3

The miracle question. Think of one problem you currently have. It has to be something (apart from physical illness) which is stopping you from moving forward in your life. Now imagine that in the night, while you were asleep, a miracle happened and the problem was removed. What would life look like for you then? What would you do in your day that you don't currently do? Link this with visualisation. Now ask yourself what the first step toward having that day would be.

Exercise 4

Get on your feet and start moving round in a space. Imagine that you're weightless and able to move without any restrictions. See what this does to the way you feel emotionally. This can be contrasted with imagining that you're moving through thick treacle. How does this affect you emotionally and physically?

Final thoughts

This chapter has highlighted the importance of visualisation and imagination in building new stories and roles. I often use this phrase with clients: If you can't see it, you can't be it. Returning to the three-act framework, we looked at the importance of knowing which act your life story is in and how to move it forward to the next act.

NINE

Build A New Role

In my work with clients, this is the point at which we stop talking about how things could change and step into the change itself. There's no need to be too detailed with the new story here; we just need a few rough brushstrokes because whatever we plan is likely to change anyway. Now is the time to move into action.

Let's look at some keys to open the mind, body, soul, heart and spirit to new roles and ways of being.

Less talk, more action

I've seen many people circle around this point of change for years. Why? Because it's easier to talk about change than to do it.

CASE STUDY – GARY

A talented businessman, Simon avoided promotion for years because he'd grown up with parents who told him that money was the root of all evil and that he should be content with little. This narrative became a block to his moving up the corporate ladder. He believed it was unethical to earn more money and have more power.

Then, after doing some visualisation work and starting to feel what it would be like to have more money, he stepped into a career change. This change propelled him into a role he previously thought was impossible to attain and dramatically changed his life.

This is where we step over the threshold into action. At this stage, we're still rehearsing new narratives and roles. But as we've discussed, the brain makes little distinction between the imagination and the real world. This is where we really start to utilise the tools of acting and theatre training. Remember, you don't need to be 'arty' or a good actor to use these tools. I've used them in one form or another to help many different kinds of people step out of habits and stories that are keeping them stuck and into the freedom to choose another way. There's some overlap here with ideas commonly used in talking therapy and coaching, but I utilise these them in a fresh way. The approach is unique, embodied and holistic.

The ideas presented in this chapter are often used in the context of group work, but they can all serve as warm-ups and exercises for individuals.

Movement

Many styles of coaching and therapy use words and thoughts as a way to change the dominant narrative and the role being played. In the world of drama, it has always been known that these changes can be achieved more quickly by focusing on the body and movement.

In Chapter 5, we discussed the *commedia dell'arte* style of acting. Letting all my movement be led by one part of my body, such as my nose, belly, knees or top of my head, made a huge difference in terms of the role I took on. If my forehead was leading, I immediately found a character who was inquisitive. If my belly led, I became more aware of greedy, libidinous impulses. This work quickly got me out of my head and into the body, where – much to my surprise – all these characters were waiting to spring into action.

Try it out! Let yourself be led round the room by different parts of the body and see what comes up.

We can quickly shift from our normal persona into roles that are quite different and yet defined. It doesn't need to take years of psychotherapy. Some change can happen instantly, and the key is how we move. This approach is linked to mime and mask work in that a focused shift in our external shape or face triggers an emotional and physical shift from our 'normal' role. These new roles can be the basis for new stories.

At drama school, I also came across the idea of the psychological gesture. This is the idea that each character we play has a signature movement that is both physical and emotional. So when I was playing a new role, I would think, *What is the movement or mannerism that sums up this role?* I'd then perform that movement. First, I'd make it as big as possible. Then I'd reduce it, smaller and smaller, until it was just an internal movement. This was a fast way to anchor into a new role and the energy inside it.

EXERCISE: What's your signature movement?

If one movement summed up the essence of the role you most play in the world now, what would it be? Would it be a spreading of the arms out wide to the world, for example, or a curling up into a little ball? Play around with this idea.

If you're not sure how to find your own gesture, stand still and start to notice the little movements that you instinctively make. Then exaggerate these and amplify them by ten. Repeat the gesture until you're familiar with it. Now think about the opposite gesture and try that out. Gradually make the gesture smaller and smaller until it's an internal state.

This exercise has two functions. It reveals the story and role inside us that we unconsciously express (and others pick up). It also allows us to try another gesture on for size. This serves as a foundation for switching out of our habitual role and narrative.

Posture

Amy Cuddy has done research into how our posture changes the way people see and respond to us. It also changes the way we feel about ourselves. She describes power poses, which are expansive movements that take up space.[12] Try some big postures out and see how they make you feel. Do you feel your status change?

When I played the dauphin in *Henry V*, I hunched over, looked at the ground and mumbled. This was the same posture I had in my everyday life. It was low status and low confidence. When I straightened, looked up and expanded my shoulders, I started to feel the character's power and status. Other actors started to pay attention when I spoke. A simple shift in posture makes a big difference to not only how we see ourselves but also how others see us. And others' reactions will often confirm our new role/narrative.

---

12   A Cuddy, *Presence*

Lean in, lean back or hold the space

When I was at drama school, my tutor pointed out that I tended to lean forward when acting. This would pull me off balance and decrease my power. Often in life we lean into other people to win their approval, show we like them or express care. Leaning in can also take the form of talking loudly and quickly and generally being overbearing. This is often rooted in a lack of self-confidence. Conversely, leaning back can be linked to being withdrawn, nervous and withholding. These are physical habits that also express old stories. Rather than going into the stories, we can change these patterns from the 'outside in' by working on posture and physicality.

The optimal position is being rooted through our feet and connected with our spine. This enables us to express ourselves without withdrawing from others or trying to force and dominate the relationship. It's a posture of power but also vulnerability. I like Brené Brown's terminology: 'Strong back, soft front'.[13]

EXERCISE: Which way do you lean?

As you go through your day, and particularly when you're talking with other people, notice if you're leaning

---

13   B Brown, 'Brené on strong backs, soft fronts, and wild hearts', Unlocking Us with Brené Brown (2020), https://open.spotify.com/episode/4bzdPR8mZr8ohiJhzkFmWt?go=1&utm_source=embed_v3&t=0&nd=1, accessed 12 May 2021

in or leaning back. If you're doing either, guide yourself back to a central position. Does this improve your breathing? Give you more power or energy?

Role

In my work with clients who want to break out of their old, habitual roles and narratives, I don't train them to be actors. And I'm not coaching people to simply shift from being in one role to another one. Even if they achieved this, who's to say they wouldn't get equally stuck in that role?

I'm much more interested in giving people the tools to become flexible enough to move between different roles and narratives at different times (having said this, I don't subscribe to the post-modern idea that we have no core identity other than the collage of roles we pick up and play given our context). This is why I recommend meditation, exercise and mindfulness – so we can sink into our bodies and hearts and find that place within where we can learn to play and be flexible again.

I see no reason why professional actors should be the only ones to benefit from these transformational exercises I'm about to outline. And if we're going to take ideas from the world of acting and drama, let's take from the best. Some directors will ask their actors to try on their characters and develop them by going out in the street as that character. Bear with me – this isn't as far out as it sounds. Have you ever left the house with a new hat or coat or haircut and felt different? Maybe people even related to you differently? Occasionally when I'm on my way back from church still wearing my collar, people will look at me differently. But more importantly, I feel different. For example, I'm less likely to pick my nose in public when I'm wearing the collar.

Embodying a character, part 1

Think of a character who is very different from you. It might help to think of film, TV or soap stars or look at images in a magazine. Then think about how that character walks and the clothes they wear. Try this role out somewhere where no one will recognise you – maybe while you're out shopping or on a walk in the countryside or in a different part of town. If you have to speak with others, such as shopkeepers, consider the way you speak. This may feel rather odd, but the purpose of the exercise is to take a trip back to the play corner and try on some different roles. As the great acting teacher Sanford Meisner put it, 'Acting is behaving truthfully under imaginary circumstances.'[14]

This isn't about permanently embodying any specific role but discovering what bubbles up to the surface.

---

14 S Meisner and D Longwell, *Sanford Meisner on Acting* (Vintage Books, 1987)

You might discover strengths and feelings that could be helpful to you in regular life. However you put together a role, however different to your 'true self' it seems, it will draw on aspects of your inner life that have always been there, even if you weren't aware of them. There's a whole range of untapped abilities, strengths and talents lying dormant inside us. Stepping into a role triggers these more quickly than years of therapy.

Working with role reminds us just how narrow the roles we play in 'normal' life are in comparison to the potential range we have within us.

Embodying a character, part 2

Now give your character different objectives. What is their aim? Are they rushing to see a sick relative? To a hot date? To meet a parent?

I have a friend who says that every meeting he has, even socially, needs to have a focus, an objective for him. This may seem calculated, but how many things do we do without any objective? We often act on the basis of unquestioned habits and patterns that are assumed to be the right way to behave. Setting a simple objective can pull us out of habits. Objectives trigger our ability to influence what's happening around us. For example, your objective might be to make a friend smile. This will lead you to speak and act in ways that will elicit this reaction, and we can practice these in role play.

EXERCISE: Role Play

For this exercise, you'll need at least one other person. Give yourself a character, maybe based around a psychological gesture or a particular body part. Then get your partner to ask you questions, which you'll answer in character. This is a great way to get deeper into a role.

Imagine the character is in a situation of conflict and must make a difficult choice. How they respond to this and the choices they make are the essence of role and plot. Visualise yourself in situations of pressure, dilemma and choice as the character. You may be surprised by the insights and solutions that the role comes up with.

Liberating ourselves from our usual habits by playing different roles can unleash a lot of new perspectives. In everyday life, we can easily get frozen or overwhelmed by dilemmas and choices. We revert to type and use the same toolkit we've used for years, whether or not it actually works. Role play frees us to come up with new ideas and new actions.

Text

So far, we've looked at improvisation as a method for living a new narrative, but written text can be a powerful point from which to jump into a new narrative, a new way of being. Some time ago, I took part in a series of dramatherapy workshops. One of the main things I remember about these workshops was how we used text. In one workshop, there were two of us, and we played different characters using the same page of text (from a play). Reading the text was like wearing a costume. We would emphasise different words or make the sentences mean different things. You can try this.

EXERCISE: Read between the lines

Take a page from a play or a screenplay and try playing all the parts. Or do this with a friend. Reading text can free us from our default patterns of speaking, thinking and moving. You don't need to know the character you're playing. In fact, you don't need to know the story of the play either. Let the words on the page lead you into expressing whatever you associate with them. You could also do this exercise by writing a page of dialogue between two characters and using this as your text.

While working in a mental-health day centre, I facilitated a play-reading group. The group's members were clients with long histories of mental illness. The stories and roles they played out were usually constrained and defined by their diagnoses, giving them a sense of powerlessness and passivity. But when reading text in this group, some clients could dramatically shift into new levels of status, power, groundedness and influence. The text drew out new aspects of their character that might have lain dormant for thirty years.

Improvisation – Mr Meisner and me

My first Meisner acting class took place in a basement studio near Covent Garden, London. It was a hot summer day, and I'd signed up for four hours in a class that I knew would take me way out of my comfort zone. This was a big step into my Act 2. I didn't know anyone else in the group, and I wasn't in control. Even today I can be quite shy, so for me this was equivalent to jumping out of a plane and hoping to God the parachute opened. We'll come back to the details of what transpired in this class shortly.

The main reason I found this class challenging and exciting was because it moved me from my head to my heart, from thinking before acting to acting and thinking simultaneously. When we're stuck in our old narratives, particularly bad ones, we tend to split thinking apart from action. Or worse, there may be a lot of thinking before any action at all. In the Meisner approach, this gap is completely closed.[15] It can almost seem that action is faster than thought. This is disorientating to a mind that likes to be in control. Moving from control and into flow is the principle that underpins improvisation.

We talked about flow in Chapter 4. It's a state of being where our ability is equal to the challenge at hand. One does not exceed the other. For example, if the challenge

---

15   S Meisner and D Longwell, *Sanford Meisner on Acting* (Vintage Books, 1987)

is great and we don't have the ability to meet it, we tend to burn out and get discouraged or even depressed. If our ability exceeds the level of the challenge, we get bored and switch off. Improvisation helps us get out of our controlling heads and into flow. This is incredibly important for any type of problem-solving.

So, back to my workshop in the sweaty basement. One of the classic exercises in the Meisner approach is the repetition game. Two people face each other, and one person says what they see in a neutral tone. This may be the colour of the other person's shirt or eyes, for example. The other person repeats what the first person has said, also in a neutral tone, and the first person keeps saying it until the second person makes an observation, and the process continues. It's so quick that there's no time to think, just react. This is one way to step out of the everyday persona and into a more intuitive state.

One of the things I like about this approach is that it makes you focus on the other person and not your own reaction. Focusing on others is an essential element of switching out of our stuck stories and roles. This is because the persona we usually enact is often based on self-defensiveness and a degree of fear of others. Improvisation breaks us free of this.

This improv approach also frees us to accept others' suggestions, rather than blocking them with a *yes but* or a *no*. This allows us to have adventures and get out of our ruts.

The yes game

The yes game is ridiculous in its simplicity. One person suggests that everyone else do something physical (and something that is physically possible in the space), such as touch a wall. Everyone else says, 'Yes, let's touch a wall', and then everyone scatters around the room to do so. Then someone else quickly suggests another movement. The aim of the game is to eliminate 'blocking'. Blocking is when someone says something such as, 'But I don't like touching walls – they have germs', or 'Why are we playing this silly game?' Blocking happens when people stop being in flow and get into their heads. Overthinking is the death of spontaneity. This is as true in life as in drama.

EXERCISE: Fast scene work

For this simple improv exercise, you need at least two characters who may or may not have a relationship with each other. But certain things must be established:

- Where the scene is taking place
- Who the characters are
- What they want

Then play the scene. It can be powerful when one character's wants (objectives) are at odds with the other character's.

There are many improv resources available – the key is to let go of control and trust the process and the people working with you. Improv is a helpful part of the overall process of stepping out of the old story and role and into something new.

Final thoughts

In this act, we looked at various aspects of writing and rehearsing a new story. You can try on different characters and ways of being and see how they feel for you. You can try out different costumes and different ways of walking and standing. You can rehearse how different objectives impact your actions and energy. The formula isn't precise because there needs to be space to play and improvise. But the exercises and ideas we've just covered in this act are a great way to rehearse living out alternative life narratives.

Next, we move to Act Three, where everything comes together into the performance of everyday life.

ACT THREE
OWN THE STAGE

TEN

Step Into Your New Story

We've arrived at the part of the process where it's time to try out the new story and the changes in your role in everyday life. This is like an actor stepping onto the stage to perform all the things they've rehearsed.

But first, most actors will go through some form of warm-up. This prepares their imaginations, voices, bodies and minds for the performance.

The warm-up

At drama school, I'd do warm-ups at the start of class or before going on stage. These were often physical, but I'd also clear my head and focus in on the role I was to play.

Today, I meditate for thirty minutes in the morning. This involves stilling my chattering thoughts and clearing my mind. I'm not trying to achieve or control or predict anything. This emptying out of ego-thinking is essential if I am to engage with divinity and find peace. But this daily practice is also essential if I am to be fluid and flexible enough to improvise my way through the day.

When people go to the gym, they're encouraged to warm up and stretch before lifting weights or doing cardio. Why shouldn't the same apply before we go 'onstage', into our day-to-day life? This is particularly true if we're adopting new stories and roles. Just as is the case at the gym, if we try to make big changes without the warm-up, we're likely to hurt ourselves.

I'm an advocate of doing three things in any warm-up. You can repeat one or all of these throughout the day:

1. Physically warm up

2. Meditate

3. Visualise

Physically warm up

To avoid being stuck in our heads, and to get into a more playful space, it is helpful to warm up the body.

There are two aspects to physically warming up. One is increasing flexibility and ease of movement. The other is building strength and stamina. The first can be achieved with practices such as yoga, the second with running and resistance training. Whatever approach you take, I'd advise putting some focus into breathing from the diaphragm.

For our narratives to really change, we need to move from being mentally busy to being physically active, hence the title of this book to *Get Unstuck* and change the script. This means physically taking on the role or persona you want. This is a conscious choice. As discussed, we all carry psychological gestures inside us that are often linked to painful pasts. Without consciously moving in another direction, we'll always slide back into default stories. We unconsciously re-enact these narratives in our bodies – in how we stand, move, breath and walk.

As mentioned, for many years, I'd walk with my eyes on the ground, collapsed in on myself. This was a re-enactment of my narrative of being invisible and fearing others' judging eyes. The only way to change default enactments is to shift to new ones. When I started working on my posture and imagined an invisible string pulling me up from the centre of my head, I immediately felt better. My breathing expanded, and I also felt more present and connected to the world around me. I didn't feel like hiding. I'd adopted what

Amy Cuddy would call a power pose, [16] and the change came about instantaneously. Years of reading and thinking about it didn't get me there. Taking action did.

As part of your daily routine, think about the story you want to tell about yourself and enact it. Don't wait to think yourself into the right feelings and then act differently. Act differently and let that change the feelings.

Meditate

This will help you to sink deeper into your core, or soul. I suggest taking an approach that allows you to empty the mind of all thought. This means entering stillness. It involves the unknown. At first this can seem daunting. Your mind will likely dart back to the security blanket of thought, worry and fear stories. But consistent meditation allows us to step back from narratives that are often rooted in trauma and speak the language of threat and fear.

Many people find it helpful to take the body-scan approach to meditation, whereby you heighten awareness of each part of the body, one at a time, and notice any feelings and thoughts as you go through this head-to-toe scan. As you notice these thoughts and feelings, simply let them pass through your awareness without trying to hold on to them or control them.

---

16   A Cuddy, *Presence*

Visualise

I recommend doing this last. This is where we build a narrative for the day ahead. Usually we apply familiar, vague and often fearful narratives to the day's events and activities. But looking ahead in this way often triggers anxiety. Instead, construct the best possible narrative for the day. If you're not sure what's going to happen, make it up. But go for the most positive, while realistic, option in your visualisation.

These three steps will help you let go of ego and control. More than this, they'll make you less susceptible to being controlled by old mindsets and ego.

Time for action

This final act is all about taking action on a daily basis. This is where the new story is embodied. It will almost never work out the way you think, but by going through the process described in this book, you'll put yourself in the best position to respond to what life throws at you. If you've done the rehearsal work detailed in Act Two and you've done the warm-up work, you'll be able to pivot into creative and new reactions to life rather than falling back into old patterns and stories. You'll be free to make choices.

We're moving into action.

You've reimagined the story you want to live. You've embodied and inhabited the roles you want to play in this story. You can now step onto the stage of your life and perform as the new you. But before you make a move or utter a line, remember that unlike in a play, you're free to improvise, make stuff up and go off script. All the preparation we've done isn't about locking you into another narrative box. It's about preparing you to be flexible enough to be a ninja in your own life. Whatever way of being you choose will be acted out in the context of relationships.

One of the keys that unlocked my self-preoccupation as an actor was focusing on the person I was speaking with. Through listening and reacting, I got out of my head and into a dialogue. In a dialogue, there is space for the other. This can really set you free to flow into your authentic energy.

The curtains have opened. You're on!

Dialogue

Being in dialogue rather than monologue is a daily practice. It can be done only with other people and will automatically keep us out of our old, default narratives. Dialogue is fundamentally a process of surrendering our position and opening up to others' narratives while not being taken over by them. This also makes me think of the 'strong back, soft front' idea.[17] Dialogue fails when we fall into others' narratives or seek to impose ours on them.

I've put dialogue at the top of the list when it comes to practicing the new narrative. It's critical to not divorce your new role and story from the roles and stories of those around you, whether at work or with family and friends. For any change to be sustainable, we need to engage with others while staying in our authenticity. This empowers us to hear others and be open to their feelings.

For much of my life, I didn't have a strong spine in relationships. I needed approval so much that I'd do and say what others wanted to hear. This was even reflected in my posture. I used to be unable to resist being pulled into others' stories and was unable to offer my own point of view.

More recently, I've worked with many couples for whom dialogue is difficult. This often happens when someone has expectations regarding how the other person is supposed to be and then can't cope when they step out of these roles. A key to breaking out of this trap is to listen to the other person and then check that you've heard accurately by repeating what they

---

17   B Brown, *Dare to Lead* (Vermillion, 2018)

said. This often reveals that someone has completely misunderstood what was said and is reacting to their own story rather than the other person.

Healthy dialogue also depends on being able to state your feelings, your thoughts, while leaving space open for the other person to influence you. I often think of this as a dance where both people can lead at different times. Dialogue is a way of building narratives with others that are flexible enough for both people to live in. This isn't only the basis for friendships but also business teams and organisations. When dialogue ends, fear and rigid stories takes over.

Living with objectives in view

Visualising the day ahead is linked with setting objectives. These aren't abstract ideas; they're tangible things that you want. Think about what you want for your day. This makes dialogue with others more intentional. For example, you might want to talk about a specific topic with someone. This is your objective. As with acting, so with life. Think about your objective and let that lead you.

These wants may involve outcomes for other people. Wanting the best for your organisation can be as motivating as wanting something for yourself.

EXERCISE: Set an objective

Think of one tangible thing you want today regarding either:

- A relationship
- Something for another person
- Finances
- An activity

Now get in touch with the feeling this want gives you. Notice the energy that comes with this want. Visualise receiving and being changed by this objective happening. Now let this go and move into your day with this intention in place. You may want to check through the day to see if this want is still in play or if it's been replaced with something else.

Final thoughts

This chapter has been like the actor in a play doing a warm-up just before they step into the spotlight. This can be like a checklist for us in our daily routine. Warming up is a process that includes the body but also the mind. So, exercise and meditation and visualisation are equally important.

ELEVEN

Stay Light On Your Feet

Finally, let's focus on what you need to do to stay light on your feet in your new story and role, regardless of what life offers you.

The cycle continues

Transforming old stories isn't a one-off process. In storytelling, the narrative starts with disruption, moves through points of escalating challenge and arrives at a final breakthrough which will change life for the better, both for the hero and those around them. But as we go through life, other disruptions will occur. Other problems will arise. Setbacks will happen. Over the course of the life of someone who is invested in transformation, there will probably be several journeys through the storytelling process.

Part of living 'on stage' and in our potential is to recognise that the process of change never stops. We cannot expect a single solution to make life work perfectly from here on out. We need a working model that can embrace suffering and setbacks and that, crucially, has a process for dealing with them.

We'll continue to react to situations based on outdated stories. Don't let this discourage you when you're facing disruption, bad feelings or upsetting events. You can always turn disruption into growth.

Embrace disruption

When I was working as an actor, every night in the theatre was different. There was always some form of disruption to react to. One night, England was playing Germany in a World Cup football match, and the game was being shown on a TV in a bar below the theatre. Every now and again the action on stage would be punctuated by a roar or horrified shouts and cursing from the depths below. We couldn't ignore this. We had to adapt. Sometimes these adaptions to the disruption improved the show.

It's the same in life. Disruption is here to stay. It's hard-wired into the fabric of our lives. It's embedded in the national and international news. We live in an unstable and turbulent world, and some disruptions may be tragic or traumatic.

One way to turn disruption from a threat into an ally is to get curious about it. Some disruptions will come in the form of obstacles to our objectives. Some will have their origins in us, some in others and some in the world around us. Rather than trying to blank them out, take a moment to ask yourself, 'What happened there?' Once, I was sitting in a coffee shop when a woman started shouting at the staff, calling them liars, and then slid off her chair and onto the floor. I tried to continue writing as if this hadn't happened, but then I saw an off-duty nurse go to the woman and, with great kindness, help her back to her chair. I realised I wasn't watching a disturbance – I was watching the enactment of love. I chose to focus on this rather than my frustration at being interrupted in my 'flow'.

So, there are two ways to respond to disruption. (I'm using the term *disruption* in the sense of life events that aren't abusive. Abuse cannot and should not be accommodated.) We can try to ignore it, or we can be hospitable to it – see what it's telling us. If we take a moment to do the latter, the disruption could turn into an opportunity for a new perspective, a new way of thinking or a chance to learn something about ourselves. Resisting or ignoring disruption is often linked with a retreat into fear or old narratives. In improvisational drama, disruption is embraced and might be seen as a new character entering the play. If you're thrown a curveball, ask yourself how it can help you grow.

The fastest way to ride the wave of disruption is to engage with it without letting it define you. Dance with it – don't cling to the wall and hope it will pass you by. This requires a sense of playfulness and freedom.

For some of us, the biggest disruptions won't come from external events but from internal stories resurfacing. My biggest disruptions tend to be things like the sudden pang of comparison when I go on Facebook and see a picture of a friend sitting on a balmy beach while I'm stuck in a coffee shop. Or when I feel left out by friends and the old wound of abandonment starts to break the surface of my heart. These disruptions of old narratives should neither be ignored nor identified with. The best way to manage them is to step further into them – in particular, to feel them in the body and perhaps imagine them as images. I find that even doing this for a minute will burst the illusionary bubble of that story and de-escalate the anxiety and fear it produces. Trying to avoid it just makes it worse. Imagination is helpful here.

Stay playful

Play will look different for everyone. As we've seen, play is the foundation of drama and role play. But for now, let's think of play as a state of being. We could describe it as being in flow. To get into this state, you need to feel relaxed and safe and okay with being silly.

EXERCISE: Get playful

To help you determine what play looks like for you, answer these questions:

- When was the last time you couldn't stop laughing? Who were you with? What were you doing?
- What activity makes you lose track of time?
- What's your most recent example of doing something just because you loved it?

Completing this exercise should help you reconnect with your playfulness. Now plan to have fun again. Don't leave it to chance. Laughing and tapping into joy is the rocket fuel you need to connect heart, mind and soul in an instant. Playfulness also helps you to stay light on your feet. If you're being pulled back into your old story, you'll probably be feeling heavy and stuck. Playfulness keeps you agile and less likely to take yourself too seriously.

Imagination boosts

One of the biggest threats to growth and transformation of narratives is fearful thoughts. We can use imagination to free ourselves from these. Sometimes

I use what I call a 'spot the monster' technique with clients. The way this works is to turn any problem or bad feeling into an image – maybe a bear, a black cloud or whatever suits the issue at hand. This imaginative leap is helpful because as soon as we imagine bad feelings as an image of something, we distance ourselves enough from them for their threat to diminish. We can then explore questions such as 'What have I done in the past that diminishes the size of the creature?' Some people find that being around others decreases stress, so this is one strategy.

Imagination has the power to lift a worry or anxiety out of us, reshape it and give us some distance from it. This can make it easier to see solutions and avoid being overwhelmed by something. As discussed, it's helpful to visualise what's coming up and see yourself overcoming any potential obstacles.

Like our bodies, our imaginations need to be warmed up daily. One way of doing this is to draw or doodle whatever comes to mind, especially when you've just woken up. This can be a great way to keep in touch with your conscious creativity. Some people also write 'daily pages'. I first became aware of this approach when I read *The Artist's Way*, by Julia Cameron.[18] It's about writing down what comes to mind without editing or censoring. This often reveals old, stuck narratives that

18 J Cameron, *The Artist's Way: A spiritual path to higher creativity* (Souvenir Press, 2020)

have been hovering just below my conscious awareness. It can be a great daily practice if you want to clear your system of unhelpful narratives at the start of the day. Equally, it can be helpful at the end of the day to capture what's been achieved and celebrate the wins.

Living in the body

I've started to dance at least once a day, usually while waiting for the kettle to boil. This does two things: it keeps me from getting stuck on what's in my head, and it helps me tap into the playful joy I need to do my work and relate well to others. In addition, movement, particularly free movement (rather than practices that follow sequences, such as yoga or tai chi) is a great way to express different facets of myself. Different kinds of music can help us connect to different characters and methods of expression. New stories and ways of being must be rooted in our physicality, not our heads.

You can also check in with yourself through mindfulness and meditation practices. Focusing on breathing is a helpful way to anchor and ground ourselves physically and emotionally. I find movement that takes me out of my comfort zone helpful in terms of mindfulness. Slow, precise movement, such as tai chi, can guide us into a shape and form that's different from what we're used to. So it's not just about getting in touch with our physicality – it's about getting in touch with a physicality that's just a little different from our normal. Actors do this every time they inhabit a new role. It keeps the body from becoming complacent and familiar with old body-shape narratives.

When you're talking with someone at work or setting the table for dinner, notice how you're moving. Is this how the new you moves? Is your movement rooted in confidence and freedom, or is it sending the message that you have the woes of the world on your shoulders?

Your internal director

Are you telling the story you want to tell?

Hopefully by this point you've started creating a more authentic story for your life and you have greater freedom to create and express different aspects of yourself with others. In time, this will become the 'new normal', so it's worth checking in with yourself occasionally to make sure you're still telling the story you want to live.

It can be helpful to step back and look at the big picture sometimes. Film directors have to get close to the details of what the actors are doing, but they also have to be able to step back and see how a scene serves the bigger story. This is an important skill for life. I certainly find it easy to spend most of my time on the day-to-day details of life that crowd in on me. Nowhere is this more apparent than in the world of social media and constant emails jockeying for attention.

You could also think of this in terms of the difference between management and leadership. Management involves efficiently climbing the ladder of success; leadership involves determining whether the ladder is leaning against the right wall.

It's incredibly easy to spend most of our energy on details and never check where we are on the map. Keep questioning yourself. Keep examining the role or character you're playing – your identity. 'Is everything I'm doing serving the story I want to tell?' 'Is this who I am?' Taking just half a day to make sure you're in the right story and role can be incredibly helpful.

Even if you're on track, ask yourself if you're finding all the potential in your story or role. It might be time to switch things up. Something I've learned from my personal trainer is that we need to change our physical challenges regularly because our bodies get used to them. Unless change keeps happening, we'll plateau and stop growing. Do you know what your 'meta objective' is? And when did you last check where you are on the road map of your big story?

All good directors try to keep their actors in flow. This means that they need to be challenged but not overly challenged, or they'll be stressed out. Conversely, they need to be operating within their skill set, but it shouldn't be too easy, or boredom will set in. It's worth checking where you are on this continuum.

Finally, the director sees the purpose of the whole story and always keeps this in mind. Some businesses and individuals have mission statements to keep them on track. I think this can be of value as long as we don't get too locked into the idea of life needing to meet certain expectations – because it never does. I find it helpful to see the director of my life as something outside me, a higher power. This isn't a passive position, as I contribute to the process of directing, but it's not all on me. As we step into our potential and authentic selves, we enter the flow of relationships both with others and our higher power.

Final thoughts

I hope the tools and inspiration in this book help you create and live a new story. And I hope that you've seen that your new story won't be completely new. It will be an awakening of aspects of yourself that have been dormant.

We don't become someone else. We become who we always were – someone who is free to make the world a better place and bring their unique flavour to the great stream of life.

The world needs you to be you because you're the only one who can play your role and live your story.

Acknowledgements

I'd like to thank the wonderful people in my life who've been such an essential part of this book's coming into being.

I've learned more than I can say from my clients and students over the years. I'll always be grateful for the trust shown me by my therapy clients and their bravery in pursuing personal transformation. The students I've taught and had dialogue with at the London School of Theology and around the world have sharpened and developed a lot of the ideas in this book. I'd also like to thank all my teachers and fellow students at Drama Studio London, University of Hertfordshire and the University of Bedfordshire. The melting pot of drama and therapy has given birth to how I work.

I'm beyond appreciative of friends who have encouraged or mentored me along different parts of my journey. Thank you to Lin Button, John Coles, Carrie and David Grant, Øyvind Aamli, David Gyasi, Azariah France-Williams, Caleb Storkey and John Lowe.

I want to express my gratitude to my amazing and endlessly patient wife, Zoe. You have always had my back and been in my corner. And last but certainly not least, thank you to my three children, Jonathan, Tamsyn and Juliet. You never cease to inspire and amaze me.

The Author

 André is a psychotherapist who has worked in Harley Street, the Priory Hospital and the NHS. He has managed an eating disorders unit, worked as a corporate coach and trained other therapists. André is a registered therapist (UKCP).

His unique approach enables clients to rewrite their life stories and create new futures for themselves. André draws on his experience as a therapist and actor to help people break out of stuck patterns. This approach can be used in relationships, business or life in general. He hosts the *Pivot Points* podcast, which can be found on iTunes, Spotify and other platforms. In this popular podcast, André speaks with celebrities and influencers about their breakthroughs and personal pivot points.

André has published a book about addiction (*Insight into Addiction* published by CWR) and several professional articles about therapy. André has written for various publications, including the *Independent* and *Metro*, and has also appeared on TV and radio as a psychological expert.

You can find André at:

- 🌐 andreradmall.com
- 🔗 andreradmall
- 🐦 @RadmallAndre
- 📷 andreradmall

Lightning Source UK Ltd.
Milton Keynes UK
UKHW022258080921
390250UK00012B/2467